perfect
cupcakes, cookies
& muffins

contents

perfect treats

Whatever the occasion or mood, if you're looking for the perfect treat, you've come to the right place. This collection of recipes covers three favorite types:

• **Cupcakes** are sweet indulgences for kids and grown-ups alike. These no-fork-required, single servings of cake are fun to make, to decorate, and to eat. Whether you're after recipes for snacks or for sophisticated desserts, this collection's variety of options, from Peanut Butter and Banana Cupcakes to After-Dinner Mint Cupcakes, is sure to satisfy your taste buds.

• **Cookies** come in different sizes, shapes, and textures, and the recipes in this book embrace and reflect their eclectic nature. Clear instructions walk you through the most common techniques: drop cookies, rolled and cut cookies, hand-formed cookies, and bar cookies. Recipes range from Toffee–Chocolate Chunk Cookies to Almond Meringues.

• **Muffins** also offer the convenience of a single-serving size. From Cider Muffins with Cinnamon-Streusel Topping to Bacon, Corn, and Onion Muffins, muffins have the versatility to satisfy a sweet tooth or a savory craving. Super simple to make, muffin recipes are an ideal choice for both beginning bakers and experienced chefs.

What's a perfect treat? You decide. Happy baking!

cupcakes

What makes the perfect cupcake?

From the standpoint of baking, it starts with a great recipe and the right equipment. This collection of kitchen-tested recipes aims to provide reliably excellent results every time. All of them have been developed specifically to work with a six-cup muffin pan. You can choose a traditional metal pan, or a silicone muffin pan to safeguard against burning. You can spoon the batter into paper cupcake liners, or foil liners, or right into the pan.

These are the technicalities. But there's another way to approach the matter of cupcake perfection, and that is from the standpoint of taste. When it comes to personal taste, there is no one perfect cupcake apart from the kind that you think achieves perfection at any particular moment. That is why this collection organizes its 26 recipes by theme, to help you choose the right cupcake to suit any occasion or any mood. Each recipe also features an assortment of special, creative "Make It Different!" hints that will help you easily achieve many more variations, expanding the possibilities this little book offers to literally hundreds of different cupcakes.

After all, every day, indeed every moment, can have its own particular perfect cupcake.

cupcake basics

Great cupcakes are so easy to make that you don't really need much in the way of instructions beyond what you'll find in each of the recipes in this book. Nevertheless, being aware of a few guidelines will increase not only your success but also the pleasure you get from the process.

● **Read and follow the recipe.** Review the ingredients and instructions before starting. Do follow all instructions to the letter; don't take shortcuts, which could affect the results.

● **Use the right equipment.** All of the recipes in this book work with a six-cup muffin pan with standard ½-cup (125-ml) cups. If using a metal muffin pan, plan to grease the cups with nonstick baking spray, butter, or shortening, or use paper or foil cupcake liners. If using a flexible silicone tray, place it on a rigid metal baking sheet to hold it steady for filling and safe, easy transfer into and out of the oven.

● **Prep ingredients in advance and measure precisely.** Before you start preparing any recipe, follow its ingredients list for specifics on how to measure and prepare each item. Have all the prepped ingredients lined up in your work area, ready to use at the right moment.

● **Have fun.** Try the recipe variations. Visit gourmet shops for pretty decorations like edible sugar flowers to make your own original creations. After all, that's what cupcakes are all about!

chocolate chip
cupcakes

Think of these as chocolate chip cookies in cupcake form, plus dollops of chocolate frosting.

● Preheat the oven to 350°F (180°C). Prepare a 6-cup standard (½-cup/125-ml) muffin pan by greasing or inserting liners.

● In a medium bowl, whisk together the flour and sugar, then add the chocolate chips. In a small mixing bowl, combine the egg, milk, melted butter, and vanilla. Add to the flour mixture and stir until just moistened. Divide among the prepared cups.

● Bake until the tops spring back when lightly tapped, 20–25 minutes. Remove from the oven and cool in the pan for 10 minutes, then transfer to a wire rack to cool.

● For the frosting, put the chocolate, cream, and butter in a heatproof bowl over but not touching a pan of simmering water. Stir gently over low heat until smooth. Chill until firm but spreadable, then pipe or spread over the cooled cupcakes.

Make It Different!

● *Use white chocolate chips instead of the semisweet (plain) and milk chocolate ones.*

● *Add a few tablespoons of roasted peanuts, pecans, or walnuts to the batter.*

● *Top the cupcakes with white chocolate frosting or Vanilla Buttercream (page 19).*

makes 6

cupcakes

1 cup (5 oz/155 g)
self-rising flour

¼ cup (2 oz/60 g) sugar

¼ cup (1½ oz/50 g) each
semisweet (plain) and milk
chocolate chips

1 egg, lightly beaten

½ cup (4 fl oz/125 ml) milk

3 tablespoons (1½ oz/45 g)
butter, melted

½ teaspoon vanilla extract
(essence)

chocolate frosting

1½ oz (45 g) semisweet
(plain) chocolate, chopped

2 tablespoons heavy
(double) cream

¾ tablespoon butter

makes 6

1 cup (4 oz/125 g) cake (soft-wheat) flour

1 teaspoon baking powder

¼ teaspoon salt

¼ cup (2 oz/60 g) unsalted butter, at room temperature

½ cup (4 oz/125 g) sugar

1 egg

½ teaspoon vanilla extract (essence)

⅓ cup (3 fl oz/80 ml) sour cream

Vanilla Buttercream (page 19)

Red food coloring

6 hard candy flowers, for decoration

vanilla sour cream
cupcakes

Look in baking supply or gourmet food shops for candy flowers to top these pretty cupcakes.

● Preheat the oven to 350°F (180°C). Prepare a 6-cup standard (½-cup/125-ml) muffin pan by greasing or inserting liners.

● In a small bowl, whisk together the flour, baking powder, and salt. In a medium bowl, using a hand-held mixer on medium speed, beat together the butter and sugar until light. Beat in the egg and vanilla until well blended. Gradually beat half of the dry ingredients into the butter mixture, then half of the sour cream; repeat with the remaining dry ingredients and sour cream.

● Divide the batter evenly among the prepared muffin cups. Bake until the tops spring back when lightly tapped, 20–25 minutes.

● Cool on a wire rack for 10 minutes, then turn out the cupcakes and cool completely on the rack. Meanwhile, make the Vanilla Buttercream, beating

in just a few drops of the red food coloring to achieve the desired pink color. Spoon this frosting into a piping bag fitted with a large star tip and, starting near each cupcake's edge, pipe it in a spiral to form a mound on top of the cupcake. Top the frosting with a hard candy flower.

Make It Different!

● *Substitute Chocolate Frosting (page 12) or any other frosting you like for the Vanilla Buttercream.*

● *Try a different flavoring extract (essence) in place of vanilla.*

● *In place of the candy flowers, decorate with crystallized violet or rose petals, or popular candies like jelly beans.*

---

peanut butter and banana cupcakes

One of the all-time most popular flavor combinations comes together in these deliciously gooey cupcakes.

● Preheat the oven to 350°F (180°C). Prepare a 6-cup standard (½-cup/125-ml) muffin pan by greasing or inserting liners.

● In a small bowl, whisk together the flour, baking powder, and salt. In a medium bowl, using a hand-held mixer on medium speed, beat together the sugar and peanut butter until light. Beat in the egg, then the mashed banana. Gradually beat in the dry ingredients just until combined. Divide the batter equally among the prepared cups.

● Bake until the tops spring back when lightly tapped, 20–25 minutes. Cool on a wire rack for 5 minutes, then turn out and cool completely.

● Meanwhile, melt the butter in a skillet over medium heat. Add the banana slices and sauté until browned, about 1 minute; turn them over and brown on the other side. Transfer to paper towels to cool.

● For the frosting, put the peanut butter in a small bowl and use a hand-held mixer on medium speed to beat until fluffy. Gradually beat in the sugar. Beat in enough of the cream to reach a spreading consistency. Stir in the peanuts.

● Spread the frosting on the cooled cupcakes. Top with banana slices.

Make It Different!

● *Substitute almond butter, cashew butter, or hazelnut (filbert) butter for the peanut butter.*

● *Cut the cupcakes horizontally in half and add a layer of Chocolate Frosting (page 12).*

● *Spoon a dollop of jelly in the middle of the batter in each cup, or on top of the frosting.*

makes 6

cupcakes

1 cup (4 oz/125 g) cake (soft-wheat) flour

1 teaspoon baking powder

¼ teaspoon salt

½ cup (4 oz/125 g) sugar

¼ cup (2½ oz/80 g) creamy peanut butter

1 egg

½ cup (4 oz/125 g) mashed ripe banana (1 small banana)

1 tablespoon butter

1 banana, sliced

chunky peanut butter frosting

¾ cup (7½ oz/235 g) creamy peanut butter

½ cup (2½ oz/75 g) confectioners' (icing) sugar

1–2 tablespoons heavy (double) cream

¼ cup (1½ oz/45 g) coarsely chopped roasted peanuts

makes 6

cupcakes

¾ cup (3 oz/90 g) cake (soft-wheat) flour

1 teaspoon baking powder

¼ teaspoon salt

¼ cup (2 oz/60 g) unsalted butter, at room temperature

¼ cup (2 oz/60 g) sugar

1 egg

½ teaspoon vanilla extract (essence)

⅓ cup (3 fl oz/80 ml) milk

¼ cup (2 oz/60 g) multicolored confetti sprinkles

vanilla buttercream

1½ cups (6 oz/190 g) confectioners' (icing) sugar

½ cup (4 oz/125 g) unsalted butter, at room temperature

½ teaspoon vanilla extract (essence)

1–2 tablespoons heavy (double) cream

vanilla rainbow
cupcakes

Mixed into the batter, a scattering of colorful confetti sprinkles makes these cupcakes extra festive.

● Preheat the oven to 350°F (180°C). Prepare a 6-cup standard (½-cup/125-ml) muffin pan by greasing or inserting liners.

● In a small bowl, whisk together the cake flour, baking powder, and salt. In a medium bowl, using a hand-held electric mixer on medium speed, cream together the butter and sugar until well blended. Beat in the egg and vanilla until light. Gradually beat in half of the flour mixture. Beat in the milk and then the remaining flour mixture until blended. Fold in half of the sprinkles. Divide the batter equally among the prepared cups.

● Bake until the tops spring back when lightly tapped, 20–25 minutes. Cool on a wire rack for 10 minutes, then turn out and cool completely.

● Meanwhile, make the Vanilla Buttercream. In a medium bowl, use a hand-held mixer on medium speed to beat together the confectioners' sugar and butter until blended. Beat in the vanilla, then beat in enough of the cream to achieve a soft consistency suitable for spreading or piping.

● Fill a pastry bag fitted with the large star tip with the Vanilla Buttercream and pipe it onto the cupcakes. Scatter the remaining sprinkles over the frosting.

> ### Make It Different!
>
> ● *Replace the confetti sprinkles with rainbow sprinkles (jimmies) both in the batter and on top.*
>
> ● *Substitute Chocolate Frosting (page 12) for Vanilla Buttercream.*
>
> ● *Instead of sprinkles on top, use shiny edible silver or gold dragées.*

pound cake cupcakes
with lemon-lime glaze

Dense, moist, and delicious, these treats gain extra flavor from a sweet citrus-flavored topping.

● Preheat the oven to 350°F (180°C).

● In a small bowl, whisk together the cake flour, baking powder, and salt. In a separate bowl, beat the eggs together with the sour cream and vanilla. In a large mixing bowl, using a hand-held mixer on medium speed, cream together the butter and sugar until well blended. Beat in about a third of the egg mixture, then half of the dry ingredients; then another third of the eggs, then the remaining dry ingredients; and finally the remaining egg mixture until completely blended.

● Divide the batter equally among 6 standard (½-cup/125-ml) greased or lined muffin cups.

● Bake until the tops spring back when lightly tapped, 20–25 minutes. Cool on a wire rack for 5 minutes.

● Meanwhile, in a small bowl, stir together the confectioners' (icing) sugar and the lemon and lime juices and zests.

● Turn out the cupcakes, place the wire rack over a sheet of waxed paper, and return them to the rack. Spoon the citrus glaze generously over the warm cupcakes, allowing some to run down the sides. Serve warm or cooled.

Make It Different!

● *Add 1 tablespoon of grated citrus zest to the cupcake batter.*

● *Substitute orange or mandarin juice and zest for some or all of the lemon or lime.*

● *Garnish the tops with thin strips of citrus zest or candied peel.*

makes 6

½ cups (6 oz/185 g) cake (soft-wheat) flour

1 teaspoon baking powder

¼ teaspoon salt

3 eggs

2 tablespoons sour cream

1 teaspoon vanilla extract (essence)

¾ cup (6 oz/185 g) unsalted butter, at room temperature

¼ cup (2 oz/60 g) sugar

1 cup (4 oz/125 g) confectioners' (icing) sugar

1½ teaspoons each freshly squeezed lemon and lime juice

1 teaspoon each grated lemon and lime zest

makes 6

½ cup (4 oz/125 g) sugar

½ cup (4 oz/125 g) butter, chopped into small pieces

¾ teaspoon vanilla extract (essence)

2 eggs

1⅓ cups (7 oz/215 g) self-rising flour, sifted

¼ teaspoon baking soda (bicarbonate of soda)

¾ cup (6 fl oz/180 ml) sour cream

⅔ cup (2⅔ oz/80 g) chopped pecans

½ teaspoon ground cinnamon

1 tablespoon plus 1 teaspoon firmly packed brown sugar

pecan coffee cake
cupcakes

An excuse for eating cupcakes in the morning, these get a velvety texture from sour cream in the batter.

● Preheat the oven to 350°F (180°C).

● In a food processor with a stainless-steel blade, combine the sugar, butter, vanilla, eggs, flour, baking soda, and sour cream. Process until smooth, 1–2 minutes.

● Distribute half of the batter evenly among the cups of a 6-cup standard (½-cup/125-ml) greased or paper-lined muffin pan.

● In a small bowl, combine the pecans, cinnamon, and brown sugar. Sprinkle half over the batter in the pan. Top with the remaining batter, then sprinkle with the remaining pecan mixture.

● Bake until the cupcakes spring back when lightly touched, 20–25 minutes. Cool in the pan for 5 minutes. Serve warm, or transfer to a wire rack to cool.

Make It Different!

● *Replace the pecans with walnuts or hazelnuts (filberts).*

● *Try crème fraîche, French-style cultured cream, in place of the sour cream.*

● *Drizzle the warm cupcakes with a simple glaze made by stirring together 1 cup (4 oz/125 g) confectioners' (icing) sugar and 1–2 tablespoons milk.*

orange zest
cupcakes

A sprinkling of finely shredded orange zest and sugar adorn these light and airy cupcakes.

● Preheat the oven to 350°F (180°C). Prepare a 6-cup standard (½-cup/125-ml) muffin pan by greasing or inserting liners.

● For the topping, in a small bowl, combine 1 teaspoon of the sugar and ½ teaspoon of the orange zest, pressing the zest into the sugar with the back of a spoon. Set aside.

● In a mixing bowl, stir together the flour, baking powder, salt, and remaining orange zest. Stir in the remaining sugar. In a small mixing bowl, combine the egg, milk, melted butter, and orange juice concentrate. Add all at once to the flour mixture and stir just until moistened.

● Divide the batter equally among the prepared cups. Sprinkle the tops with the sugar-orange mixture. Bake until the tops spring back when lightly tapped, 20–25 minutes. Cool on a wire rack for 10 minutes, then turn out and cool completely.

Make It Different!

● *Add 1 teaspoon ground ginger to the dry ingredients for the batter.*

● *Spoon a dollop of orange marmalade into the center of the batter in each cup.*

● *Top each cupcake with Chocolate Frosting (page 12), which tastes great with orange.*

makes 6

¼ cup (2 oz/60 g) plus
1 teaspoon sugar

1½ teaspoons finely
shredded orange zest

¾ cup (3 oz/90 g) cake
(soft-wheat) flour

¾ teaspoon baking powder

Pinch of salt

1 egg, beaten

¼ cup (2 fl oz/60 ml) milk

2 tablespoons melted butter

1 tablespoon frozen orange
juice concentrate, thawed

makes 6

¼ cup (2 oz/60 g) butter

¼ cup (2 oz/60 g) light molasses (golden syrup)

¾ cup (4 oz/125 g) self-rising flour

½ cup (2½ oz/75 g) whole wheat (wholemeal) flour

1 tablespoon ground ginger

¼ teaspoon baking soda (bicarbonate of soda)

3 tablespoons brown sugar

1 egg, lightly beaten

½ cup (4 fl oz/125 ml) milk

2 tablespoons candied (glacé) ginger, chopped, plus more for garnish

1 small ripe pear, peeled, cored, and chopped

½ cup (2 oz/65 g) confectioners' (icing) sugar, sifted

gingerbread pear
cupcakes

An old-time favorite cake translates well into cupcakes, especially with the addition of sweet, juicy pear.

● Preheat the oven to 350°F (180°C). Prepare a 6-cup standard (½-cup/125-ml) muffin pan by greasing or inserting liners.

● In a small saucepan over low heat, gently melt half of the butter with all but ½ teaspoon of the molasses. Stir to combine, then set aside to cool.

● In a large mixing bowl, sift together the flours, ¾ tablespoon ground ginger, and baking soda. Stir in the brown sugar. In a small mixing bowl, combine the egg, milk, and cooled butter and molasses mixture. Add all at once to the flour mixture along with the candied ginger and chopped pear. Stir just until moistened. Divide among the prepared cups.

● Bake until the tops spring back when lightly tapped, 20–25 minutes. Cool on a wire rack for 5 minutes, then turn out and cool completely.

● In a small saucepan over low heat, melt the remaining butter and molasses. Add the confectioners' (icing) sugar and remaining ground ginger and stir until melted and smooth. Spread immediately over the cupcakes and garnish with more candied ginger.

Make It Different!

● *Try chopped apple in place of the pear.*

● *Add a tiny dash of grated nutmeg to the dry ingredients with the ground ginger.*

● *Serve the cupcakes warm with vanilla ice cream instead of frosting.*

double-decker
carrot cupcakes

Wholesome and delicious, these easy cupcakes have an extra layer of luscious frosting spread just underneath their crowns.

● Preheat the oven to 350°F (180°C).

● In a medium mixing bowl, whisk together the flour, baking powder, salt, and spices. In a separate bowl, using a hand-held electric mixer on medium speed, beat together the eggs, sugars, and oil. Stir into the dry ingredients just until blended. Stir in the carrot and chopped walnuts.

● Divide the batter equally among the cups of a 6-cup standard (½-cup/125-ml) greased or paper-lined muffin pan. Bake until the tops spring back when tapped lightly, 20–25 minutes. Cool on a wire rack for 5 minutes, then turn out the cupcakes and cool completely.

● Meanwhile, make the Cream Cheese Frosting. In a mixing bowl, use a hand-held mixer on medium speed to beat together the butter, cream cheese, sugar, and vanilla until smooth.

● With a serrated knife, cut each cupcake in half horizontally. Spread some of the Cream Cheese Frosting over the cut surface of the bottom halves. Replace the top halves, and frost them generously.

Make It Different!

● *Substitute chopped pecans for the walnuts.*

● *Add a few drops of orange food coloring to the frosting.*

● *Top each cupcake with a roasted or candied walnut half.*

makes 6

cupcakes

1 cup (5 oz/155 g)
all-purpose (plain) flour

1 teaspoon baking powder

¼ teaspoon salt

1 teaspoon ground
cinnamon

¼ teaspoon grated nutmeg

2 eggs

½ cup (3½ oz/105 g)
packed brown sugar

½ cup (4 oz/125 g) sugar

½ cup (4 fl oz/125 ml)
vegetable oil

1½ cups (7 oz/215 g)
grated carrot

½ cup (2 oz/60 g) chopped
walnuts

cream cheese frosting

¼ cup (2 oz/60 g) butter,
at room temperature

4 ounces (125 g)
cream cheese, at room
temperature

1 cup (4 oz/125 g)
confectioners' (icing) sugar

½ teaspoon vanilla
extract (essence)

makes 6

5 tablespoons
(2½ oz/75 g) butter

1 cup (5 oz/155 g)
self-rising flour

⅔ cup (2⅔ oz/80 g) grated
dried (desiccated) coconut

⅓ cup (3 oz/90 g) sugar

1 egg, lightly beaten

½ cup (4 fl oz/125 ml) milk

1 teaspoon grated
lemon zest

2 tablespoons lemon juice

¼ cup (1½ oz/45 g)
all-purpose (plain) flour

Vanilla Buttercream
(page 19)

⅔ cup (2⅔ oz/80 g)
sweetened shredded
coconut

lemon coconut
cupcakes

The richness of coconut and the zesty taste of lemon are natural partners in these festive cupcakes.

● Preheat the oven to 350°F (180°C). Prepare a 6-cup standard (½-cup/125-ml) muffin pan by greasing or inserting liners. Melt 1½ tablespoons of the butter; put the remainder in the refrigerator to chill.

● In a large mixing bowl, sift the self-rising flour. Stir in ½ cup (2 oz/60 g) of the grated coconut and ¼ cup (2 oz/60 g) of the sugar. Make a well in the center. In a small bowl, combine the egg, milk, melted butter, zest, and juice. Add all at once to the flour mixture and stir just until moistened. Divide evenly among the prepared cups.

● Put the all-purpose flour and remaining grated coconut and sugar in a small bowl. Cut the chilled butter into cubes and rub it into the dry ingredients with your fingertips until the mixture resembles coarse crumbs. Spoon evenly over the cupcakes.

● Bake until the tops are springy when lightly tapped, 20–25 minutes. Cool in the pan for 5 minutes, then turn out to cool completely. Spread the Vanilla Buttercream on top and sprinkle evenly with the coconut shreds, pressing them gently into the buttercream.

Make It Different!

● *For an even more intense coconut flavor, use the thick layer of cream from the top of a can of coconut milk in place of the melted butter in the batter.*

● *Use orange zest and juice in place of the lemon.*

● *Top the icing with strips of candied (glacé) lemon peel.*

black and white
cupcakes

A favorite deli-style cookie translates perfectly into cupcakes topped with two different icings.

● Preheat the oven to 350°F (180°C). Prepare a 6-cup standard (½-cup/125-ml) muffin pan by greasing or inserting liners.

● In a medium bowl, whisk together the sugar, sour cream, oil, egg, and vanilla. Sift in the flour, cocoa, and baking soda. Stir until blended. Divide the batter equally among the prepared cups.

● Bake until the tops spring back when lightly tapped, 20–25 minutes. Cool on a wire rack for 10 minutes, then turn out to cool completely.

● Meanwhile, make the icings. For the Chocolate Icing, combine the cream and corn syrup in a small, heavy saucepan and bring to a simmer over medium-low heat. Remove from the heat and stir in the chocolate chips until smooth. Let cool until it reaches a thick but fluid spreading consistency.

For the White Icing, in a small bowl, stir together the sugar, vanilla, and enough of the cream to form a smooth icing.

● Spread each icing over half of the top of each cupcake. Let stand until set, about 1 hour.

Make It Different!

● *Use white chocolate chips in place of the semisweet in the Chocolate Icing.*

● *Color the White Icing with a few drops of food coloring.*

● *Scatter white chocolate chips over the brown icing and dark chocolate chips over the white icing.*

makes 6

cupcakes

½ cup (4 oz/125 g) sugar

½ cup (4 fl oz/125 ml) sour cream

⅓ cup (3 fl oz/80 ml) vegetable oil

1 egg

½ teaspoon vanilla extract (essence)

¾ cup (3 oz/90 g) cake (soft-wheat) flour

⅓ cup (1 oz/30 g) unsweetened cocoa powder

¾ teaspoon baking soda (bicarbonate of soda)

chocolate icing

2 tablespoons heavy (double) cream

2 teaspoons light corn syrup

⅓ cup (1⅔ oz/50 g) semisweet (plain) mini chocolate chips

white icing

½ cup (2 oz/60 g) confectioners' (icing) sugar

¼ teaspoon vanilla extract (essence)

1–2 tablespoons heavy (double) cream

makes 6

1 cup (5 oz/155 g)
self-rising flour

¼ teaspoon baking soda
(bicarbonate of soda)

3 tablespoons unsweetened
cocoa powder

¼ cup (2 oz/60 g) sugar

¼ cup (1½ oz/50 g) milk
chocolate chips

½ cup (3 oz/90 g)
semisweet (plain) chocolate
chips

1 egg, lightly beaten

¾ cup (6 fl oz/180 ml) milk

2 tablespoons butter,
melted

triple-chocolate
cupcakes

Three different sources of rich chocolate flavor make these easy cupcakes three times as delicious for chocolate lovers.

• Preheat the oven to 350°F (180°C). Prepare a 6-cup standard (½-cup/125-ml) muffin pan by greasing or inserting liners.

• In a mixing bowl, whisk together the flour, baking soda, and cocoa. Stir in the sugar, all of the milk chocolate chips, and half of the semisweet (plain) chips. In a small bowl, mix the egg, milk, and butter. Add all at once to the flour mixture and stir until just moistened.

• Divide the batter evenly among the prepared cups. Bake until the tops spring back when lightly touched, 20–25 minutes. Cool in the pan for 5 minutes, then turn out onto a wire rack to cool completely.

• Meanwhile, put the remaining chocolate chips in a microwave-safe bowl and melt in short bursts in the microwave. Stir until smooth. Using a teaspoon, swirl the melted chocolate thickly over the top of each cupcake.

Make It Different!

• *Substitute white chocolate chips for some or all of the milk chocolate chips in the batter.*

• *Use white chocolate instead of semisweet chips for the melted chocolate icing.*

• *While the melted chocolate icing is still soft, decorate it with sprinkles (jimmies).*

chocolate cherry
cupcakes

Whether fresh, bottled, or canned, cherries show their special affinity for chocolate in these cupcakes.

● Preheat the oven to 350°F (180°C). Prepare a 6-cup standard (½-cup/125-ml) muffin pan by greasing or inserting liners.

● In a mixing bowl, whisk together the flour and allspice. Stir in the almonds, sugar, chocolate chips, and cherries. In a small mixing bowl, combine the egg, butter, and buttermilk. Add all at once to the flour mixture and stir just until moistened. Divide the batter evenly among the prepared cups.

● Bake until the tops spring back when lightly tapped, 20–25 minutes. Cool on a wire rack for 5 minutes, then turn out and cool completely.

Make It Different!

● *In the early summer season, look for beautiful fresh gold-and-red Rainier cherries to use in the batter.*

● *Replace the ground almonds in the batter with ground hazelnuts (filberts).*

● *Spread the cupcakes with Chocolate Frosting (page 12).*

makes 6

1 cup (5 oz/155 g)
self-rising flour

½ teaspoon ground allspice

2 tablespoons ground
almonds

2½ tablespoons brown
sugar

½ cup (3 oz/90 g)
semisweet (plain)
chocolate chips

½ cup (3 oz/90 g)
bottled or canned sweet
red cherries, pitted and
drained, or same quantity
fresh sweet cherries, pitted

1 egg, lightly beaten

3 tablespoons butter,
melted

⅓ cup (3 fl oz/80 ml)
buttermilk

makes 6

1 can (20 oz/600 g) pineapple tidbits

¼ cup (2 oz/60 g) packed light brown sugar

½ cup (4 oz/125 g) unsalted butter, melted

1 cup (4 oz/125 g) cake (soft-wheat) flour

½ teaspoon baking powder

¼ teaspoon salt

2 egg yolks

⅓ cup (3 oz/90 g) sugar

Softly whipped cream, optional

6 maraschino cherries with stems

pineapple upside-down
cupcakes

A favorite old-fashioned novelty cake becomes an exciting new treat when you prepare it in the form of individual cupcakes.

● Preheat the oven to 350°F (180°C).

● Drain the pineapple, reserving ½ cup (4 fl oz/ 125 ml) of its juice. In the bottom of each cup of a 6-cup standard (½-cup/125-ml) silicone muffin pan or a greased metal muffin pan, neatly arrange 7 pineapple pieces in a circle. (Reserve any leftover pineapple pieces for another use.) Sprinkle each arrangement with 2 teaspoons brown sugar. Drizzle 2 teaspoons melted butter into each cup. Set aside.

● In a small bowl, whisk together the flour, baking powder, and salt. In a separate bowl, using a hand-held electric mixer on medium speed, beat together the egg yolks, sugar, and remaining butter until light. Gradually beat in half of the dry ingredients. Beat in the reserved pineapple syrup, then the remaining dry ingredients until well blended. Spoon the batter evenly into the prepared cups. Bake until the centers spring back when touched lightly, 20–25 minutes. Cool in the pan on a wire rack for 10 minutes. Then, carefully invert onto a baking sheet or tray to unmold, rearranging any pineapple bits as necessary. Transfer with a spatula to individual serving dishes and serve warm or at room temperature, garnishing each with a dollop of whipped cream if desired and a cherry.

Make It Different!

● *Add 2 tablespoons chopped macadamia nuts to the batter.*

● *Substitute other canned fruit in syrup such as apricots, pitted cherries, or peaches.*

● *Sprinkle sweetened coconut shreds over the pineapple before adding the batter.*

red-hot red velvet
cupcakes

Cocoa powder, cinnamon candies, and red food coloring give these cupcakes devilish flavor and color.

- Preheat the oven to 350°F (180°C). Prepare a 6-cup standard (½-cup/125-ml) muffin pan by greasing or inserting liners.

- In a medium bowl, whisk together the flour, sugar, cocoa powder, 2 teaspoons of the crushed candies, the baking soda, and the salt. Set aside. In a medium bowl, using a hand-held mixer on medium speed, lightly beat the egg. Beat in the buttermilk, vinegar, oil, food coloring, and vanilla. Beat in the dry ingredients until thoroughly blended. Divide the batter equally among the prepared cups.

- Bake until the tops spring back when lightly tapped, 20–25 minutes. Cool on a wire rack for 10 minutes, then turn out and cool completely.

- Place the frosting in a pastry bag fitted with the large plain tip. Pipe dollops of frosting onto the cupcakes. Sprinkle with the remaining crushed candies.

Make It Different!

- *Use ground cinnamon in place of the crushed candies in the batter.*

- *Substitute Vanilla Buttercream (page 19) or Chocolate Frosting (page 12) for the Cream Cheese Frosting.*

- *Decorate the cupcakes with red-hot cinnamon-flavored jellybeans.*

makes 6

¾ cup (4 oz/125 g) unbleached all-purpose (plain) flour

½ cup (4 oz/125 g) sugar

¼ cup (¾ oz/20 g) unsweetened cocoa powder

1 small box (1 oz/30 g) hot cinnamon-flavored candies, crushed

½ teaspoon baking soda (bicarbonate of soda)

½ teaspoon salt

1 egg

⅓ cup (3 fl oz/80 ml) buttermilk

½ teaspoon distilled white vinegar

⅓ cup (3 fl oz/80 ml) vegetable oil

5 teaspoons red food coloring

½ teaspoon vanilla extract (essence)

Cream Cheese Frosting (page 28)

makes 6

mexican streusel topping

3 tablespoons almond meal

3 tablespoons all-purpose (plain) flour

1 tablespoon packed light brown sugar

2 tablespoons unsalted butter, chilled

½ disk (about 1½ oz/45 g) Mexican chocolate, roughly chopped

cupcakes

½ cup (3 oz/90 g) almond meal

½ cup (2 oz/60 g) cake (soft-wheat) flour

½ teaspoon baking soda (bicarbonate of soda)

¼ teaspoon salt

¼ cup (2 oz/60 g) unsalted butter

1 disk (about 3 oz/90 g) Mexican chocolate, finely chopped

2 eggs, separated

¼ cup (2 oz/60 g) sugar

¼ cup (2 fl oz/60 ml) sour cream

mexican chocolate
streusel cupcakes

Look for cinnamon-spiced Mexican chocolate in the ethnic foods aisle, at Latino markets, or online.

• First, prepare the topping. In a small bowl, combine the almond meal, flour, and brown sugar. Rub the butter into the mixture until it resembles coarse meal. Stir in the chocolate. Refrigerate.

• Preheat the oven to 350°F (180°C). Prepare a 6-cup standard (½-cup/125-ml) muffin pan by greasing or inserting liners.

• For the cupcakes, in a small bowl, whisk together the almond meal, flour, baking soda, and salt. In a saucepan, melt the butter over low heat. Stir in the chocolate until smooth. Set aside.

• In a medium bowl, using a hand-held electric mixer on medium speed, beat the egg yolks and sugar together until thick and pale yellow. Gradually beat in the cooled chocolate mixture. Gradually beat in half of the dry ingredients, then the sour cream, and then the remaining dry ingredients.

• Beat the egg whites until they hold stiff peaks. With a rubber spatula, gently fold about a third of the whites into the batter. Then, in two more batches, fold in the remaining whites, blending completely.

• Divide the batter among the prepared muffin cups. Crumble the streusel on top. Bake until the tops spring back when lightly tapped, 25–30 minutes. Cool on a wire rack for 5 minutes, then turn out and cool completely. Serve warm or cooled.

Make It Different!

• *Add 1 teaspoon of instant espresso coffee granules to the yolk mixture.*

• *Include a tiny pinch of pure red chile powder for an intriguing hint of heat.*

• *Look for piloncillo, robust-tasting unrefined Mexican brown sugar, to use in the streusel.*

white chocolate raspberry cupcakes

The tang of raspberries counterpoints white chocolate's creamy richness in these decadent treats.

● Preheat the oven to 350°F (180°C). Prepare a 6-cup standard (½-cup/125-ml) muffin pan by greasing or inserting liners.

● In a small saucepan over low heat, melt half the white chocolate chips with the butter, stirring gently until smooth. Set aside to cool.

● In a mixing bowl, sift the flour. Stir in the sugar and remaining white chocolate chips. In a small mixing bowl, combine the egg, the milk, and the melted butter and chocolate mixture. Add all at once to the flour mixture together with the raspberries. Stir until just moistened. Divide the batter evenly among the prepared cups.

● Bake until the tops spring back when lightly tapped, 20–25 minutes. Cool on a wire rack for 5 minutes, then turn out. Serve warm, dusted with sifted confectioners' (icing) sugar.

Make It Different!

● *Substitute milk chocolate or semisweet (plain) chocolate chips for the whole white chocolate chips stirred into the batter.*

● *Add 1 teaspoon vanilla or almond extract (essence) to the batter.*

● *Top the cupcakes with Chocolate Frosting (page 12), substituting white chocolate for the regular chocolate in that recipe.*

makes 6

½ cup (3 oz/90 g) white chocolate chips

2 tablespoons butter

1 cup (5 oz/155 g) self-rising flour

¼ cup (2 oz/60 g) sugar

1 egg, lightly beaten

½ cup (4 fl oz/125 ml) milk

¾ cup (3 oz/90 g) fresh or frozen raspberries

Confectioners' (icing) sugar, for dusting

makes 6

½ cup (3 oz/90 g) chopped dates

⅔ cup (5 oz/155 g) brown sugar

⅓ cup (3 oz/90 g) butter

⅔ cup (5 fl oz/160 ml) water

½ teaspoon baking soda (bicarbonate of soda)

½ teaspoon vanilla extract (essence)

¾ cup (4 oz/125 g) self-rising flour

¼ cup (1½ oz/45 g) whole wheat (wholemeal) flour

¼ cup (1 oz/30 g) chopped pecans

1 egg, lightly beaten

¼ cup (2 fl oz/60 ml) heavy (double) cream

warm date-nut cupcakes
with caramel sauce

Served still warm from the oven and dripping with their easily prepared rich sauce, these cupcakes taste absolutely decadent.

- Preheat the oven to 350°F (180°C).

- Put the dates, half of the brown sugar, ¼ cup (2 oz/60 g) of butter, and the water in a medium saucepan. Stir over low heat until the butter has melted. Still over low heat, bring to a boil and boil for 2 minutes. Remove from the heat, cool slightly, then stir in the baking soda and vanilla. Set aside.

- In a large mixing bowl, sift together the flours. Stir in the pecans.

- Add the beaten egg to the cooled date mixture, then add all at once to the flour mixture and stir just until moistened. Divide equally among the cups of a 6-cup standard (½-cup/125-ml) greased or paper-lined muffin pan. Bake until the tops spring back when lightly tapped, 20–25 minutes.

- To make the Caramel Sauce, put the remaining brown sugar and butter and the cream in a small saucepan. Stir over low heat until the sugar has dissolved. Bring to a low boil and boil for 1 minute. Let the cupcakes cool in the pan for 5 minutes, then brush with a little of the caramel sauce. Remove from the pan and serve warm with the remaining hot Caramel Sauce.

Make It Different!

- *Substitute chopped walnuts for the pecans.*

- *Stir a little grated lime zest into the warm Caramel Sauce.*

- *After spooning on the remaining Caramel Sauce, add a dollop of whipped cream to each serving.*

passion fruit
cupcakes

Sweet and tangy passion fruit gives both the batter and the icing of these simple cupcakes an exotic tropical personality.

● Preheat the oven to 350°F (180°C). Prepare a 6-cup standard (½-cup/125-ml) muffin pan by greasing or inserting liners.

● In a large mixing bowl, mix together the flour and sugar. In a small mixing bowl, combine the egg, milk, 1 oz (30 g) of the melted butter, and all but ½ tablespoon of the passion fruit pulp. Add all at once to the flour mixture and stir just until moistened. Divide evenly among the prepared cups.

● Bake until the tops spring back when lightly tapped, 20–25 minutes. Cool on a wire rack in the pan for 5 minutes, then turn out to cool completely.

● For the icing, sift the confectioners' (icing) sugar into a small bowl. Add the remaining melted butter and enough of the remaining passion fruit pulp to give the icing a smooth, spreadable consistency. Spread the icing over the cooled cupcakes and allow it to set before serving.

Make It Different!

● *Although passion fruit seeds are edible, you can strain them out of the pulp if you prefer.*

● *Substitute puréed ripe mango pulp for the passion fruit in the batter and icing.*

● *Add an extra tropical touch by topping the icing with bits of candied (glacé) pineapple.*

makes 6

1 cup (5 oz/155 g)
self-rising flour

⅓ cup (2⅓ oz/75 g)
superfine (castor) sugar

1 egg, lightly beaten

¼ cup (2 fl oz/60 ml) milk

3 tablespoons (1½ oz/45 g)
butter, melted

¼ cup (2 fl oz/60 ml) plus
1½ tablespoons passion
fruit pulp including seeds
(about 3 ripe passion fruit)

½ cup (2 oz/65 g)
confectioners' (icing) sugar

makes 6

2 tablespoons butter

3 tablespoons honey

1 cup (5 oz/155 g)
self-rising flour

¼ teaspoon baking powder

½ teaspoon ground
cinnamon

½ teaspoon ground ginger

½ teaspoon mixed baking
spices

½ teaspoon ground
cardamom

¾ cup (3½ oz/105 g) plus
2 tablespoons slivered
almonds

1 egg, lightly beaten

⅓ cup (3 fl oz/90 ml) milk

6 sugar cubes, roughly
crushed

honey and spice
cupcakes

Almonds and sugar cubes make a crunchy topping for adult cupcakes that children will like, too.

● Preheat the oven to 350°F (180°C). Prepare a 6-cup standard (½-cup/125-ml) muffin pan by greasing or inserting liners.

● In a small saucepan, melt the butter and honey together over low heat. Set aside to cool. In a large mixing bowl, whisk together the flour, baking powder, and spices. Set aside. In a food processor, finely grind a scant ½ cup (2½ oz/75 g) of the almonds. Stir them into the dry ingredients and make a well in the center. In a small mixing bowl, combine the egg, milk, and butter-honey mixture. Add all at once to the dry ingredients and stir just until moistened. Divide the batter evenly among the prepared cups. Sprinkle the tops with the remaining almonds and the sugar cubes, lightly pressing down.

● Bake until the tops spring back when lightly tapped, 20–25 minutes. Cool in the pan on a wire rack for 5 minutes. Serve warm, or turn out onto the rack to cool completely.

Make It Different!

● *Substitute coarsely chopped hazelnuts (filberts) for the almonds in the batter and topping.*

● *Use crushed brown sugar cubes in place of the white sugar cubes.*

● *Drizzle the warm cupcakes with the Caramel Sauce from the recipe for Warm Date-Nut Cupcakes (page 47).*

chocolate and candied ginger cupcakes

Candied ginger and walnuts bring the flavor of a sophisticated confection to these easy cupcakes.

• Preheat the oven to 350°F (180°C). Prepare a 6-cup standard (½-cup/125-ml) muffin pan by greasing or inserting liners.

• In the top pan of a double boiler, combine 1 tablespoon of the cream with the chocolate and stir over (not touching) simmering water until combined. Stir in 3 tablespoons of the butter and set aside to cool. In a mixing bowl, using an electric mixer on medium-high speed, beat the egg and sugar until pale. Stir into the chocolate mixture alternately with the flour, baking soda, two-thirds of the ginger, and the walnuts.

• Divide the batter evenly among the prepared cups. Bake until the tops spring back when lightly tapped, 20–25 minutes. Cool in the pan on a wire rack for 5 minutes, then turn out and cool completely.

• For the icing, in a small saucepan combine the remaining ginger, 2 tablespoons of the remaining cream, and the brown sugar. Bring to a boil, stirring frequently, then reduce the heat and simmer for 10 minutes. Remove from the heat and whisk in the remaining butter. Refrigerate for 10 minutes. With an electric mixer on medium-high speed, beat the remaining cream until soft peaks form. Gently fold into the cooled mixture. Spread or pipe over the cupcakes.

Make It Different!

• *Use pecans in place of the walnuts.*

• *Decorate the frosting with extra candied (glacé) ginger and cocoa powder.*

• *Substitute Vanilla Buttercream (page 19) for the frosting in the recipe.*

makes 6

½ cup (4 fl oz/125 ml)
heavy (double) cream

½ cup (3 oz/90 g) plus
1 tablespoon semisweet
(plain) chocolate chips

¼ cup (2 oz/60 g) butter

1 egg

⅓ cup (3 oz/90 g) plus
1 tablespoon sugar

1 cup (5 oz/155 g)
self-rising flour, sifted

¼ teaspoon baking soda
(bicarbonate of soda)

⅓ cup (2 oz/60 g) candied
(glacé) ginger, chopped

⅓ cup (1½ oz/45 g)
plus 1 tablespoon
chopped walnuts

¼ cup (2 oz/60 g) firmly
packed brown sugar

makes 6

1 egg

1 tablespoon plus 1
teaspoon sugar

¼ cup (1½ oz/45 g)
all-purpose (plain) flour

¼ teaspoon baking powder

2 tablespoons flaked
(dessicated) coconut

1 tablespoon butter, melted

2 tablespoons raspberry
jam

Confectioners' (icing)
sugar, for dusting

coconut and raspberry
cupcakes

Hidden in its center, each of these little gems contains a delicious spoonful of raspberry jam.

• In a mixing bowl, using a hand-held electric mixer on medium-high speed, beat the egg and sugar until the mixture is thick and pale and forms a ribbon when the beaters are lifted out. In a separate bowl, whisk together the flour and baking powder. With a rubber spatula, fold about half of the flour mixture into the egg mixture; then fold in half of the coconut; and, finally, repeat with the remainder of each. Fold in the melted butter. Cover the bowl and chill in the refrigerator for 25 minutes.

• Meanwhile, preheat the oven to 400°F (200°C). Prepare a 6-cup standard (½-cup/125-ml) muffin pan by greasing or inserting liners.

• Distribute half of the batter evenly among the prepared cups. Spoon 1 scant teaspoon of jam into the center of each cup. Cover with the remaining batter. Bake until the tops spring back when lightly tapped, 15–20 minutes. Turn out onto wire racks to cool completely.

• Before serving, dust the cupcakes with confectioners' (icing) sugar.

> **Make It Different!**
>
> • *Try other flavors of jam, such as strawberry, blueberry, apricot, or your favorite marmalade.*
>
> • *In place of jam, try lemon curd.*
>
> • *Instead of dusting sugar on top, try Vanilla Buttercream (page 19) or Lemon-Lime Glaze (page 20).*

chocolate truffle
cupcakes

These rich little cakes contain a double dose of chocolate, making them as rich and sweet as the candies for which they are named.

- Preheat the oven to 400°F (200°C). Prepare a 6-cup standard (½-cup/125-ml) muffin pan by greasing or inserting liners.

- In a mixing bowl, use a hand-held electric mixer on medium-high speed to beat the butter and sugar together until light and fluffy. Add the egg and beat well. In another bowl, whisk together the flour, cocoa powder, and baking powder. In alternate batches, stir the melted chocolate, dry ingredients, and milk into the butter mixture. Distribute the batter among the prepared cups.

- Bake until the tops spring back when lightly tapped, about 20 minutes. Cool in the pan for 5 minutes, then turn out onto a wire rack to cool completely. Serve warm or cool, topped with Chocolate Glaze and candies.

Make It Different!

- *For extra-decadent results, embed a small chocolate truffle candy in the center of the batter in each cup before baking.*

- *Top the cupcakes with Cream Cheese Frosting (page 28).*

- *Instead of the glaze, simply dust the cupcakes with confectioners' (icing) sugar.*

makes 6

¼ cup (2 oz/60 g) butter

⅓ cup (3 oz/90 g) sugar

1 egg

1 cup (5 oz/155 g) self-rising flour

1 tablespoon unsweetened cocoa powder

½ teaspoon baking powder

3⅓ oz (100 g) bittersweet (dark) chocolate, melted

½ cup (4 fl oz/125 ml) milk

2 batches Chocolate Glaze (page 63)

Chocolate candies, for decoration

makes 6

⅔ cup (4 oz/120 g)
all-purpose (plain) flour

1½ teaspoons baking
powder

¼ teaspoon ground
cinnamon

Pinch of baking soda
(bicarbonate of soda)

1 tablespoon plus 2
teaspoons packed brown
sugar

3 tablespoons cream
cheese

1 egg, lightly beaten

¼ cup (2 fl oz/60 ml) milk

1½ tablespoons butter,
melted

¼ teaspoon vanilla extract
(essence)

⅓ cup (1⅓ oz/40 g)
raspberries

Confectioners' (icing) sugar,
for serving

raspberry cream
cupcakes

The perfect elegant yet easy ending for a party, this recipe works well with fresh or frozen berries.

• Preheat the oven to 350°F (180°C). Prepare a 6-cup standard (½-cup/125-ml) muffin pan by greasing or inserting liners.

• In a mixing bowl, whisk together the flour, baking powder, cinnamon, and baking soda. Stir in the brown sugar. Using a pastry blender, cut in the cream cheese until the mixture resembles pea-sized crumbs. In a small bowl, combine the egg, milk, melted butter, and vanilla. Add all at once to the flour mixture and stir just until moistened. Fold in the berries. Divide the mixture evenly among the prepared cups.

• Bake until the tops spring back when lightly tapped, 20–25 minutes. Cool in the pan on a wire rack for 10 minutes, then turn out and cool completely. Before serving, dust lightly with confectioners' sugar.

Make It Different!

• *Substitute fresh or frozen blackberries or boysenberries for the raspberries.*

• *Top with a white chocolate frosting, made using the Chocolate Frosting recipe (page 12).*

• *Purée a few raspberries, strain out the seeds, and combine with confectioners' sugar to make a raspberry glaze for the cupcakes.*

fruit and chocolate chip
cupcakes

Like little fruitcakes with the addition of chocolate, these treats travel well in packed lunches.

● In a mixing bowl, use a hand-held electric mixer on medium-high speed to beat the eggs and sugar until thick and pale, about 5 minutes. With a rubber spatula, fold in all of the remaining ingredients. Cover and refrigerate for 25 minutes.

● Meanwhile, preheat the oven to 400°F (200°C). Prepare a 6-cup standard (½-cup/125-ml) muffin pan by greasing or inserting liners.

● Distribute the batter evenly among the prepared cups. Bake until the tops spring back when lightly tapped, about 20 minutes. Cool in the pan for 2–3 minutes before turning out onto a wire rack to cool completely. Serve warm or cool.

Make It Different!

● *Replace the currants with dates or figs.*

● *Try adding hazelnuts (filberts), walnuts, or pecans in place of the almonds.*

● *For a traditional fruitcake flavor, add 1 teaspoon rum extract (essence) to the batter.*

makes 6

2 eggs

⅓ cup (3 oz/90 g) sugar

⅔ cup (4 oz/120 g) all-purpose (plain) flour

½ teaspoon baking powder

⅓ cup (3 oz/90 g) butter, melted

2½ tablespoons chopped dried apricots

1½ tablespoons finely chopped candied (glacé) cherries

½ tablespoon dried currants

½ tablespoon finely chopped blanched almonds

¼ cup (1½ oz/50 g) milk chocolate chips

½ tablespoon chopped candied (glacé) ginger

makes 6

cupcakes

¾ cup (3 oz/90 g) semisweet (plain) chocolate chips

6 tablespoons (3 oz/90 g) unsalted butter

½ teaspoon peppermint extract (essence)

½ cup (2 oz/60 g) cake (soft-wheat) flour

2 tablespoons unsweetened cocoa powder

2 eggs, separated

½ cup (4 oz/125 g) sugar

⅛ teaspoon salt

white chocolate mint icing

2 ounces (60 g) white chocolate, chopped

1 tablespoon heavy (double) cream

½ teaspoon peppermint extract (essence)

chocolate glaze

⅔ cup (4 oz/120 g) semisweet (plain) chocolate chips

2 tablespoons heavy (double) cream

6 chocolate after-dinner mints, for garnish

after-dinner mint
cupcakes

These cupcakes feature the sophisticated flavors of a treat typically enjoyed with a good cup of coffee.

● Preheat the oven to 350°F (180°C). Prepare a 6-cup standard (½-cup/125-ml) muffin pan by greasing or inserting liners.

● For the cupcakes, in a small saucepan over very low heat, melt the chocolate and butter. Stir in the peppermint and set aside. In a medium bowl, whisk together the flour and cocoa. In another bowl, with an electric mixer on medium speed, beat the egg yolks and half of the sugar until pale. Stir in the chocolate and butter mixture. In a clean bowl, with clean beaters, beat the egg whites and salt to soft peaks. Beat in the remaining sugar until stiff peaks form. Stir the flour mixture into the chocolate mixture. With a rubber spatula, fold in the egg whites in three batches. Divide the batter among the prepared cups. Bake 20–25 minutes. Cool on a wire rack for 10 minutes, then turn out and cool completely.

● Meanwhile, make the icing. In a double boiler, melt the white chocolate and cream together. Stir in the peppermint. Cool to room temperature.

● Remove the cupcake liners. With a serrated knife, cut the crown from each cupcake. Spread some icing on the bottom half. Replace the crown. Refrigerate 30 minutes.

● For the glaze, in a saucepan, heat the chocolate and cream over low heat until the chocolate is almost melted. Remove from the heat and stir until smooth. Cool until it's at room temperature but still fluid. Drizzle over each cupcake. Decorate with after-dinner mints and leave until glaze sets.

> **Make It Different!**
>
> ● *Use the Red-Hot Red Velvet Cupcakes batter (page 40), omitting the cinnamon candies.*
>
> ● *Switch the positions of the icing and glaze.*
>
> ● *Decorate with crushed candy-cane pieces.*

cookies

What's your idea of the perfect cookie? Chewy oatmeal or gooey chocolate chip? Crisp shortbread or airy meringues? Or maybe one day it's pralines, and the next you can't get enough citrus squares.

This book has all those options covered and more. Nearly three dozen kitchen-tested recipes are organized by the technique used to make them:

• **Drop cookies** are the simplest cookies to make: just spoon mounds of soft dough onto a baking sheet and put it in the oven. Classic favorites, such as chocolate chip cookies, reside in this group. Sturdy drop cookies are great on the go—in lunch boxes or picnic baskets.

• **Rolled cookies** are slightly more involved. Roll out the dough thinly, cut it into shapes using cookie cutters or a knife, and bake. Whether cut into snowflakes, gingerbread people, or hearts, the dough will keep its shape.

• **Hand-shaped cookies**, such as rolled-up wedges or biscotti logs, can be formed by hand. They can also be piped through a pastry bag or extruded through a cookie press.

• **Bar cookies and brownies** start as batters that are poured or spread into a pan and can be cut into individual servings after they bake.

Try them all. Each time you can refine your definition of a perfect cookie (or two or three).

cookie basics

Cookies are simple and delicious treats, crowd-pleasers that are accessible even to the novice baker. That said, following a few basic principles can help you turn a good cookie into a great one.

• **Read and follow the recipe.** Make sure you read through the whole recipe once before beginning. Follow the directions carefully, without shortcuts, to get the best results.

• **Use the right equipment.** Baking cookies requires a simple baking sheet, or, for bar cookies and brownies, a pan. A nonstick or silicone sheet or pan can minimize the need for greasing beforehand. The equipment you use to prepare your dough is also important. Use liquid measuring cups for liquid ingredients and dry measuring cups for dry ingredients. Before you begin to bake, make sure you have any specialized pieces of equipment you might need, such as a grater for lemon zest.

• **Prep ingredients in advance and measure precisely.** Take your ingredients out and make sure you have everything for each stage of the recipe before beginning. Ingredients should usually be at room temperature for the best results. Pay attention to whether you'll need to take a few extra steps to prepare an ingredient—if you need to sift flour, for example, do so before you start mixing. Measure dry ingredients with the "spoon and sweep" method: Use a spoon to fill the cup to overflowing, then level the top with a knife.

• **Have fun.** Whether you decide to stick to old favorites or try out new recipes with creative twists, cookies are always a perfect dessert.

makes 18 cookies

Vegetable oil cooking spray
for greasing

3½ cups (14 oz/420 g)
sweetened flaked coconut

1 cup (4 oz/120 g) sliced
(flaked) almonds

½ cup (4 fl oz/125 ml)
sweetened condensed milk

½ teaspoon almond extract
(essence)

2 large egg whites

1 tablespoon sugar

1 pinch salt

4 oz (125 g) chopped
semisweet (plain) or
bittersweet chocolate

coconut-almond
drops

- Preheat the oven to 350°F (180°C). Grease 2 large cookie sheets with cooking spray.

- Pour 1½ cups (6 oz/180 g) of the coconut and the almonds onto an ungreased rimmed baking sheet and mix well. Toast them in the oven, stirring occasionally, until golden brown, about 12 minutes. Immediately transfer the coconut-almond mixture to a large bowl to cool. Leave the oven on.

- To the bowl with the cooled coconut mixture, add the remaining 2 cups (8 oz/240 g) coconut, the condensed milk, and almond extract and mix well. In an impeccably clean and dry bowl, combine the egg whites, sugar, and salt. Using an electric mixer with clean beaters on high speed, beat until soft peaks form. Gently fold the egg white mixture into the coconut mixture using a rubber spatula.

- Using a large spoon, drop the dough into 2-inch (5-cm) mounds onto the prepared cookie sheets, spacing them 2 inches (5 cm) apart. Bake until the cookies are golden brown, about 10 minutes, then transfer to wire racks and let cool completely.

- Add the chocolate pieces to a heatproof bowl. Place the bowl over a pan of simmering water, taking care that the bowl does not touch the water. Heat, stirring frequently, until the chocolate is melted and smooth. Remove from the heat.

- Line 2 cookie sheets with waxed paper. Dip the bottoms of the cookies into the chocolate coating and place, chocolate side down, on the lined baking sheets. Refrigerate the cookies until the chocolate is set. Store in an airtight container at cool room temperature for up to 4 days.

fruity oatmeal
walnut cookies

makes 42 cookies

1 cup (8 oz/250 g) unsalted butter at room temperature

1 cup (7¾ oz/220 g) golden brown sugar, firmly packed

¾ cup (6 oz/185 g) sugar

1 large egg

2 teaspoons vanilla extract (essence)

1½ cups (7½ oz/235 g) all-purpose (plain) flour

1 teaspoon baking soda (bicarbonate of soda)

1 teaspoon ground cinnamon

½ teaspoon ground cloves

¼ teaspoon salt

1 pinch freshly grated nutmeg

3 cups (9 oz/270 g) quick-cooking rolled oats

1 cup (3 oz/90 g) chopped dried apples

1 cup (4 oz/125 g) dried cranberries

1 cup (4½ oz/125 g) chopped walnuts

● Preheat the oven to 375°F (190°C). Line 2 cookie sheets with parchment (baking) paper.

● In a bowl, combine the butter, brown sugar, and sugar. Using an electric mixer on medium-high speed, beat the mixture until light and fluffy, about 3 minutes. Beat in the egg and vanilla.

● In another bowl, sift together the flour, baking soda, cinnamon, cloves, salt, and nutmeg. Add the flour mixture to the butter mixture and stir with a wooden spoon just until blended. Add the oats, apples, cranberries, and walnuts and mix thoroughly but gently. Drop the dough by tablespoonfuls onto the prepared cookie sheets, spacing the mounds about 2 inches (5 cm) apart.

● Bake until the edges of the cookies are golden brown, about 14 minutes. Set the baking sheets on wire racks and let the cookies cool on the sheets for 1 minute, then carefully transfer the cookies to the racks and let cool completely. Store between layers of waxed paper in an airtight container in the refrigerator for up to 2 weeks.

walnut chocolate chunk cookies

makes 36 cookies

Vegetable oil cooking spray
for greasing

1 cup (8 oz/250 g) unsalted butter
at room temperature

1 cup (7¾ oz/220 g) golden brown
sugar, firmly packed

1 teaspoon vanilla extract (essence)

1 large egg

1 tablespoon orange zest, finely
grated

1 cup (5 oz/155 g) all-purpose
(plain) flour

½ teaspoon ground cinnamon

½ teaspoon baking powder

¼ teaspoon salt

3 cups (9 oz/270 g) rolled oats

1 cup (4½ oz/125 g) chopped
walnuts

6 oz (185 g) bittersweet or
semisweet (plain) chocolate,
chopped

● Preheat the oven to 350°F (180°C). Grease 2 cookie sheets with cooking spray.

● In a bowl, combine the butter, brown sugar, and vanilla. Using an electric mixer on high speed, beat the mixture until light and fluffy. Add the egg and orange zest and beat until incorporated.

● In another bowl, sift together the flour, cinnamon, baking powder, and salt. Add the flour mixture to the butter mixture and beat on low speed until well mixed. Add the oats, walnuts, and chocolate and mix well with a wooden spoon. Drop rounded tablespoonfuls of the dough onto the prepared baking sheets, spacing the mounds 2 inches (5 cm) apart.

● Bake until the cookies are golden brown, about 17 minutes. Transfer to wire racks to cool. Store in an airtight container at room temperature for up to 1 week.

toffee–chocolate chunk cookies

● Preheat the oven to 375°F (190°C). Have ready 2 ungreased cookie sheets.

● In a large bowl, combine the brown sugar, butter, and vanilla. Using an electric mixer on high speed, beat the mixture until light and fluffy. Beat in the egg.

● In another bowl, sift together the flour, baking soda, and salt. Add the flour mixture to the butter mixture and mix on low speed just until blended. Add the chocolate pieces and chopped toffee and mix with a wooden spoon until incorporated. Drop the dough by heaping teaspoonfuls onto the cookie sheets, spacing the mounds about 2 inches (5 cm) apart.

● Bake for 5 minutes. Switch the pan positions and rotate each sheet by a half turn, then continue to bake until the cookies are golden brown, about 5 more minutes. Transfer the cookies to wire racks to cool. Store in an airtight container at room temperature for up to 4 days.

makes 42 cookies

¾ cup (6 oz/185 g) golden brown sugar, firmly packed

½ cup (4 oz/125 g) unsalted butter, at room temperature

1 teaspoon vanilla extract (essence)

1 large egg

1¼ cups (5 oz/155 g) all-purpose (plain) flour

½ teaspoon baking soda (bicarbonate of soda)

¼ teaspoon salt

6 oz (185 g) semisweet (plain) chocolate, cut into ⅓-inch (1-cm) pieces

1 cup (5 oz/150 g) chocolate-covered toffee candy bar such as Heath Bar, chopped

chocolate-almond
florentines

makes 36 cookies

1 cup (4 oz/120 g) sliced (flaked) almonds

½ cup (4 fl oz/125 ml) plus 2 tablespoons heavy (double) cream

½ cup (4 oz/125 g) sugar

¼ cup (2 oz/60 g) dark brown sugar, firmly packed

2 tablespoons unsalted butter, plus extra for greasing

¼ cup (1½ oz/45 g) all-purpose (plain) flour

1 tablespoon grated orange zest

2 teaspoons grated lemon zest

4½ oz (140 g) semisweet (plain) chocolate, chopped

½ oz (15 g) unsweetened chocolate, chopped

● Preheat the oven to 350°F (180°C). Spread the almonds on a rimmed baking sheet and toast in the oven, stirring occasionally, until lightly browned, about 8 minutes. Cool the nuts on a plate. Leave the oven on.

● In a heavy saucepan, warm the cream, sugars, and butter over medium heat, stirring constantly with a wooden spoon, until the sugars dissolve and the butter melts. Add the nuts, flour, and orange and lemon zests. Turn the heat to high. Stir constantly. When the mixture boils, remove from the heat.

● Line 2 rimmed baking sheets with aluminum foil and lightly butter the foil. Working in 2 batches, drop the batter by rounded teaspoonfuls onto the prepared baking sheets (the batter will spread a bit), spacing the cookies at least 2 inches (5 cm) apart. Bake until the cookies are deep golden brown, about 8 minutes. Lift off the foil, with the cookies in place, and transfer to a wire rack to cool. Line the baking sheets with fresh foil, butter the foil, and shape and bake the remaining cookies. While the cookies are cooling, line the baking sheets with fresh foil. Carefully peel the cookies off the foil and place, smooth side up, on the newly covered baking sheets.

● Add both chocolates to a heatproof bowl placed over (not touching) simmering water. Warm, stirring frequently, until the chocolate is melted and smooth. Remove from the heat. Using a knife, spread the chocolate over the flat side of each cookie and place on the lined baking sheets, chocolate side up. Refrigerate until the chocolate sets, about 20 minutes. Store in an airtight container in the refrigerator for up to 2 weeks.

classic southern
pralines

makes 36 pralines

3 cups (24 oz/750 g) sugar

3½ cups (14 oz/420 g) pecan halves

1⅓ cups (11 fl oz/330 ml) buttermilk

6 tablespoons unsalted butter

¼ teaspoon salt

1 teaspoon vanilla extract (essence)

½ teaspoon almond extract (essence)

1½ teaspoons baking soda (bicarbonate of soda)

● Line 2 cookie sheets with waxed paper.

● In a large, heavy saucepan combine the sugar, pecan halves, buttermilk, butter, and salt. Warm over low heat, stirring occasionally, until the sugar is completely dissolved, about 10 minutes. Take care that the mixture does not boil up to this point, or it could affect the texture of the pralines. Insert a candy thermometer into the mixture. Raise the heat to medium high and bring the mixture to a boil, stirring occasionally; avoid scraping any hardened candy mixture from the sides of the saucepan. Cook until the candy thermometer reads 236°F–239°F (113°C–115°C), the "soft-ball stage," about 15 minutes.

● Remove the pan from the heat and stir in the vanilla and almond extracts. Carefully add the baking soda, which will cause the mixture to become foamy. Beat rapidly with a wooden spoon to cool the mixture, about 6 minutes; it will thicken and lose some of its shine. Working quickly, scoop up a heaping tablespoon of the mixture and use another tablespoon to push the mixture onto the lined cookie sheets. Let the pralines stand at room temperature until firm, about 1 hour. Store between layers of waxed paper in an airtight container for up to 10 days.

chewy apple-oatmeal
cookies

makes 24 cookies

Vegetable oil cooking spray
for greasing

$\frac{1}{2}$ cup (4 oz/125 g) plus
2 tablespoons unsalted butter,
at room temperature

1 cup (7$\frac{3}{4}$ oz/220 g) plus
2 tablespoons golden brown
sugar, firmly packed

1 large egg

2 tablespoons whole
(full-cream) milk

$\frac{3}{4}$ teaspoon vanilla extract
(essence)

1$\frac{1}{2}$ cups (4$\frac{1}{2}$ oz/135 g)
old-fashioned rolled oats

1$\frac{1}{2}$ cups (7$\frac{1}{2}$ oz/230 g)
all-purpose (plain) flour

$\frac{3}{4}$ teaspoon baking soda
(bicarbonate of soda)

$\frac{1}{4}$ teaspoon salt

1 cup (4 oz/125 g) tart apple,
peeled, cored, and chopped

1 cup (3 oz/90 g) dried apple,
chopped

● Preheat the oven to 350°F (180°C). Grease 2 cookie sheets with cooking spray.

● In a large bowl, combine the butter and brown sugar. Using an electric mixer on high speed, beat until light and fluffy. Add the egg, milk, and vanilla and beat until very fluffy, about 2 minutes.

● In a bowl, stir together the oats, flour, baking soda, and salt. Add the flour mixture to the butter mixture and mix on low speed until well blended. Add the fresh and dried apples and mix on low speed until combined.

● Drop the dough by rounded tablespoonfuls onto the prepared cookie sheets, spacing the mounds about 2 inches (5 cm) apart. Bake until the cookies are golden brown, about 15 minutes. Transfer the cookies to wire racks to cool completely. Store in an airtight container in the refrigerator for up to 4 days.

Variation: Caramel-Glazed Apple-Oatmeal Cookies

● To make the Caramel Glaze, in a small, heavy saucepan combine 8 oz (250 g) soft caramel candies and $\frac{1}{4}$ cup (2 fl oz/60 ml) water. Warm over low heat, stirring constantly, until the caramels melt and the mixture is smooth. Remove from the heat. Using the tines of a fork, slowly drizzle the hot caramel glaze over the cookies. Let the cookies stand until the glaze cools and hardens, about 30 minutes.

black forest
cookies

makes about 2 dozen cookies

$\frac{1}{2}$ cup (4 oz/125 g) plus
2 tablespoons unsalted butter,
at room temperature

$\frac{3}{4}$ cup (6 oz/185 g) dark brown
sugar, firmly packed

1 teaspoon vanilla extract (essence)

1 large egg

1 cup (5 oz/155 g) all-purpose
(plain) flour

$\frac{3}{4}$ teaspoon baking powder

$\frac{1}{8}$ teaspoon baking soda
(bicarbonate of soda)

$\frac{1}{8}$ teaspoon salt

8 oz (250 g) semisweet chocolate,
cut into $\frac{1}{2}$-inch pieces (about
1$\frac{1}{2}$ cups)

6 oz (185 g) dried sour cherries,
chopped (about 1$\frac{1}{2}$ cups)

● Preheat the oven to 350°F (180°C). Have ready 2 ungreased cookie sheets.

● In a large bowl, combine the butter, brown sugar, and vanilla. Using an electric mixer on high speed, beat until the mixture is light and fluffy. Add the egg and beat until incorporated.

● In another bowl, sift together the flour, baking powder, baking soda, and salt. Add the flour mixture to the butter mixture and mix on low speed just until blended. Add the chocolate and cherries and mix on low speed until incorporated.

● Drop the batter by slightly rounded tablespoonfuls onto the cookie sheets, spacing the mounds about 2 inches (5 cm) apart. Bake until the cookies are golden brown, about 16 minutes. Transfer the cookies to wire racks to cool. Store in an airtight container at room temperature for up to 4 days.

makes 30 cookies

4 oz (125 g) unsweetened chocolate, chopped

¼ cup (2 oz/60 g) unsalted butter

4 large eggs

2 cups (16 oz/500 g) sugar

1 teaspoon vanilla extract (essence)

1½ cups (7½ oz/235 g) all-purpose (plain) flour

½ cup (1½ oz/45 g) unsweetened cocoa powder, preferably Dutch-process

2 teaspoons baking powder

¼ teaspoon salt

1½ cups (9 oz/280 g) miniature semisweet (plain) chocolate chips

½ cup (2 oz/65 g) confectioners' (icing) sugar

chocolate crinkle
cookies

● Add the unsweetened chocolate and butter to a heatproof bowl placed over (not touching) a pan of simmering water. Warm, stirring often, until the butter and chocolate melt and the mixture is smooth. Remove the bowl from the pan and let the mixture cool slightly.

● In a large bowl, combine the eggs, sugar, and vanilla. Using an electric mixer on medium speed, beat until the mixture is light in color and thick, about 3 minutes. Add the melted chocolate mixture and stir with a wooden spoon or beat on low speed until blended.

● In a bowl, stir together the flour, cocoa powder, baking powder, and salt. Add the flour mixture to the chocolate mixture and beat on low speed until blended. Add the chocolate chips and stir with a wooden spoon until incorporated. Cover the bowl with plastic wrap and refrigerate until the dough is firm enough to roll into balls, about 2 hours.

● When you're ready to bake, preheat the oven to 325°F (165°C). Line 2 cookie sheets with parchment (baking) paper. Sift the confectioners' sugar into a bowl.

● Roll a rounded tablespoonful of dough between your palms into a $1\frac{1}{2}$-inch (4-cm) ball, then roll the ball in the confectioners' sugar to coat it completely. Place on a prepared cookie sheet. Repeat to shape and coat the remaining dough, spacing the balls 3 inches ($7\frac{1}{2}$ cm) apart on the cookie sheets. Press each ball down slightly so that it stays in place on the cookie sheet.

● Bake 1 sheet of cookies at a time, until the tops are puffed and crinkled and feel firm when lightly touched, about 15 minutes. Let the cookies cool on the baking sheets for 5 minutes, then use a spatula to transfer the cookies to wire racks to cool completely. Store in an airtight container at room temperature for up to 3 days.

molasses spice
cookies

makes about 30 cookies

½ cup (4 oz/125 g)
trans-fat-free vegetable shortening
(vegetable lard), plus more for
greasing

¼ cup (20 oz/60 g) unsalted butter,
at room temperature

1 cup (7 oz/220 g) firmly
packed dark brown sugar

1 large egg

¼ cup (3 oz/85 g) dark molasses

2 teaspoons grated orange zest

2 cups (10 oz/305 g) all-purpose
(plain) flour

2 teaspoons baking soda
(bicarbonate of soda)

2 teaspoons ground ginger

1½ teaspoons ground cinnamon

1 teaspoon ground cloves

1 teaspoon salt

Sugar for coating

● In a large bowl, combine the shortening, butter, and brown sugar. Using an electric mixer on high speed, beat until the mixture is light and fluffy. Add the egg, molasses, and orange zest and beat until blended.

● In another bowl, sift together the flour, baking soda, ginger, cinnamon, cloves, and salt. Gradually add the flour mixture to the shortening mixture and mix on low speed just until blended. Cover and refrigerate the dough until it is firm, at least 1 hour or up to overnight.

● Preheat the oven to 350°F (180°C). Lightly grease 2 cookie sheets. Pour some sugar for coating into a shallow bowl.

● With dampened hands, shape the dough into 1¼-inch (3-cm) balls; you should have about 30 balls. Roll each ball in sugar to coat evenly. Arrange the sugar-coated balls on the prepared cookie sheets, spacing them about 2 inches (5 cm) apart.

● Bake until the cookies are pale golden and cracked on top, about 12 minutes; the cookies will still be soft. Let the cookies cool on the cookie sheets on wire racks for about 1 minute. Use a spatula to transfer the cookies to the wire racks to cool completely. Store in an airtight container at room temperature for up to 1 week.

toffee shortbread
cookies

makes about 16 cookies

$\frac{1}{2}$ cup (2 oz/60 g) pecans

1 cup (5 oz/155 g)
all-purpose (plain) flour

$\frac{1}{3}$ cup (2$\frac{1}{2}$ oz/75 g) golden brown
sugar, firmly packed

2$\frac{1}{2}$ tablespoons cornstarch
(cornflour)

$\frac{1}{8}$ teaspoon salt

$\frac{1}{2}$ cup (4 oz/125 g) chilled unsalted
butter, cut into $\frac{1}{2}$-inch (12 mm)
pieces

$\frac{3}{4}$ teaspoon vanilla extract
(essence)

$\frac{1}{3}$ cup (1$\frac{2}{3}$ oz/50 g) chocolate-
covered toffee candy bar such as
Heath Bar, finely chopped

Sugar for sprinkling

● Preheat the oven to 350°F (180°C). Have ready 2 ungreased cookie sheets.

● In a food processor, process the pecans with the flour until finely chopped, taking care not to overprocess them. Add the brown sugar, cornstarch, and salt and process until well blended. Add the butter and vanilla and pulse just until the mixture resembles coarse crumbs. Add the toffee and pulse until just incorporated.

● Transfer the dough to a large sheet of waxed paper. Use your hands to form the dough into a disk, then top with a second sheet of waxed paper. Using a rolling pin, roll out the dough through the waxed paper to a thickness of $\frac{1}{4}$ inch (6 mm). Use a 3-inch (7$\frac{1}{2}$-cm) round cookie cutter to cut out as many rounds as you can from the dough. Gather up the scraps, roll out the dough again, and cut out additional rounds. Transfer the rounds to the baking sheets. Sprinkle the cookies with sugar.

● Bake until the shortbread turns light golden, about 20 minutes. Transfer the cookie sheets to wire racks and let the shortbread cool on the sheets for 5 minutes. Use a spatula to transfer the shortbread to the wire racks to cool completely. Store in an airtight container at room temperature for up to 5 days.

peekaboo
heart cookies

• In a food processor, process the walnuts and 1 cup (5 oz/155 g) of the flour until the nuts are finely ground; take care not to overprocess. Set aside. In a bowl, combine the butter and confectioners' sugar. Using an electric mixer on medium speed, beat until the mixture is light and fluffy, about 4 minutes. Add the egg yolks one at a time, beating well after each addition. Add the walnut mixture, the remaining flour, and the cornstarch and beat on low speed until incorporated. Divide the dough into 4 equal portions and wrap each with plastic wrap. Refrigerate for at least 2 hours or overnight.

• Preheat the oven to 325°F (165°C). Grease 2 large cookie sheets with cooking spray. Have ready two heart-shaped cookie cutters, $2\frac{1}{2}$ inches (6 cm) and $1\frac{1}{2}$ inches (4 cm) in diameter, respectively.

• Lightly flour a work surface and place one dough disk on top of the flour. Use a rolling pin to roll out the dough into a round about $\frac{1}{4}$ inch (6 mm) thick. Use the large cookie cutter to cut out as many heart "bases" as you can from the dough. Transfer half of the hearts to a prepared cookie sheet. Using the small cookie cutter, cut out a heart from the center of each of the remaining heart cutouts, creating heart "frames." Transfer the heart frames to the second prepared cookie sheet. Gather up and re-roll the smaller hearts and the scraps, then cut out an even number of additional heart bases and frames. Repeat with the remaining dough portions.

• Bake until the cookies are just golden, about 15 minutes for the bases and 12 minutes for the frames. Cool completely on wire racks.

• Using a fine-mesh sieve, dust the heart frames with confectioners' sugar. Spread a small amount of jam over the heart bases. Place the sugar-dusted frames on top of the jam-topped heart bases, lining up the edges. Store in an airtight container at cool room temperature for up to 3 days.

makes about 48 cookies

2 cups (8 oz/250 g)
walnuts, toasted (see
page 100) and cooled

2½ cups (12½ oz/390 g)
all-purpose (plain) flour

1 cup (8 oz/250 g) unsalted
butter, at room temperature

1 cup (4 oz/125 g)
confectioners' (icing) sugar,
plus extra for dusting

2 large egg yolks

½ cup (2 oz/60 g)
cornstarch (cornflour), sifted

Vegetable oil cooking spray
for greasing

Raspberry jam

hazelnut ginger
cookies

makes about 36 cookies

½ cup (2½ oz/75 g) hazelnuts
(filberts)

2 cups (10 oz/315 g)
all-purpose (plain) flour

¾ cup (6 oz/185 g) golden brown
sugar, firmly packed

¼ cup (2 oz/60 g) unsalted butter,
at room temperature

¼ cup (2 oz/60 g) trans-fat-free
vegetable shortening (vegetable
lard), at room temperature, plus
more for greasing

¼ cup (3 oz/85 g) light molasses

1 large egg

2¼ teaspoons ground ginger

1½ teaspoons ground cinnamon

1 teaspoon ground cloves

½ teaspoon salt

½ teaspoon baking soda
(bicarbonate of soda)

1 tablespoon sugar

● Preheat the oven to 350°F (180°C). Spread the nuts on a rimmed baking sheet and toast, stirring occasionally, until golden brown with skins pulling away, about 10 minutes. Place the warm nuts in a clean kitchen towel. Rub the towel vigorously to remove the skins. Let the nuts cool. Using a food processor, finely chop the nuts. Add ¼ cup (½ oz/45 g) of the flour and ¼ cup (2 oz/60 g) of the brown sugar and process to a powder; set aside.

● In a large bowl, combine the butter, shortening, and the remaining brown sugar. Using an electric mixer on high speed, beat until the mixture is light and fluffy. Add the molasses and egg and beat until incorporated.

● In another bowl, sift together the remaining flour, ginger, cinnamon, cloves, salt, and baking soda. Using an electric mixer on low speed, blend the flour mixture, the nut mixture, and the butter mixture. Divide the dough in half. Wrap each half in plastic wrap and chill until firm, at least 1 hour.

● Preheat the oven to 350°F (180°C). Grease 2 cookie sheets. Lightly dust 1 portion of the dough at a time with flour and place between 2 sheets of waxed paper. Roll to ¼ inch (6 mm) thickness, then remove the top sheet. Using a 2½-inch (6.5-cm) scalloped round cookie cutter, cut out rounds and place on the prepared cookie sheets, about ½ inch (12 mm) apart. Gather up, roll, and cut the dough scraps. Sprinkle the rounds with sugar.

● Bake until the cookies have firm edges and golden bottoms, about 12 minutes. Cool on a wire rack. Store the cookies in an airtight container at room temperature for up to 3 weeks.

chocolate peanut butter
thumbprint cookies

makes about 48 cookies

½ cup (4 oz/125 g) trans-fat-free vegetable shortening (vegetable lard), at room temperature, plus more for greasing

9 tablespoons unsalted butter, at room temperature

1 cup (8 oz/250 g) sugar, plus extra for coating

1 large egg

2 tablespoons whole (full-cream) milk

¼ teaspoon almond extract (essence)

1¾ cups (9 oz/280 g) all-purpose (plain) flour

⅔ cup (2 oz/60 g) unsweetened cocoa powder, preferably Dutch-process

1 teaspoon baking soda (bicarbonate of soda)

½ teaspoon baking powder

½ teaspoon salt

¾ cup (6 oz/185 g) creamy peanut butter

¾ teaspoon vanilla extract (essence)

½ cup (2 oz/65 g) confectioners' (icing) sugar

● Preheat the oven to 350°F (180°C). Grease 2 cookie sheets. In a large bowl, combine the shortening, 6 tablespoons of the butter, and the sugar. Using an electric mixer on high speed, beat until light and fluffy. Add the egg, milk, and almond extract and beat until incorporated, about 2 minutes.

● In another bowl, sift together the flour, cocoa powder, baking soda, baking powder, and salt. Add the flour mixture to the butter mixture and mix on low speed just until blended. Set aside.

● To make the filling, in a food processor, combine the peanut butter, remaining 3 tablespoons butter, and vanilla and process until smooth. Add the confectioners' sugar and pulse to blend; set aside.

● Using damp hands, pick up a small portion of dough and roll it between your palms to form a 1-inch (2½-cm) ball. Roll the ball in sugar to coat evenly. Continue to roll the dough into balls and coat them in sugar; you will have about 48 balls. As you work, place the balls on the prepared cookie sheets, spacing them at least 2 inches (5 cm) apart. Using your thumb, make a large indentation in the center of each ball.

● Bake until the cookies are puffed and slightly cracked, about 12 minutes. Remove the cookies from the oven and drop about 1 teaspoon of the filling in the indentation of each cookie. Let the cookies cool on the cookie sheets for 1 minute, then use a spatula to transfer them to wire racks to cool completely. Store in an airtight container in the refrigerator for up to 3 days.

chocolate-dipped orange zest cookies

makes about 24 cookies

1½ cups (7½ oz/235 g) all-purpose (plain) flour

½ cup (4 oz/125 g) sugar

¼ cup (1 oz/30 g) cornstarch (cornflour)

1 tablespoon plus 1 teaspoon orange zest, grated

¼ teaspoon salt

¾ cup (6 oz/185 g) chilled unsalted butter, cut into pieces

½ teaspoon vanilla extract (essence)

4 oz (125 g) chopped semisweet (plain) or bittersweet chocolate

● Preheat the oven to 350°F (180°C). Have ready 2 ungreased cookie sheets.

● In a food processor, process briefly the flour, sugar, cornstarch, orange zest, and salt. Add the butter and vanilla. Pulse a few times, until the mixture resembles fine meal, then process just until moist clumps form.

● Transfer the mixture to a large sheet of waxed paper. Using your hands, press the dough together to form a flat disk. Top with a second sheet of waxed paper. Roll out the dough to a thickness of about ¼ inch (6 mm) and remove the top sheet of waxed paper. Using a 2½- to 3-inch (6½- to 7½-cm) cookie cutter, cut out rounds. Using a metal spatula, transfer the rounds to the cookie sheets, spacing them about ½ inch (12 mm) apart. Gather up, roll, and cut the dough scraps.

● Bake until the cookies are just beginning to brown, about 14 minutes. Transfer the cookie sheets to wire racks for 5 minutes. Then use a spatula to transfer the cookies to the racks to cool completely.

● Add the chocolate pieces to a heatproof bowl. Place the bowl over (not touching) a pan of simmering water. Heat, stirring frequently, until the chocolate is melted and smooth. Remove from the heat.

● Line a cookie sheet with waxed paper. Dip the cooled cookies in the chocolate, coating one-half of each cookie. Arrange the coated cookies in a single layer on the lined cookie sheet. Refrigerate until the chocolate sets. Store in an airtight container in the refrigerator for up to 1 week.

gingerbread people
cookies

makes about 20 cookies

cookie dough

¾ cup (6 oz/185 g) unsalted butter, at room temperature

¾ cup (6 oz/185 g) golden brown sugar, firmly packed

¼ cup (3 oz/85 g) light molasses

2 large egg yolks

2⅓ cups (12 oz/375 g) all-purpose (plain) flour

2 teaspoons ground cinnamon

2 teaspoons ground ginger

1 teaspoon ground allspice

½ teaspoon baking soda (bicarbonate of soda)

¼ teaspoon ground cloves

¼ teaspoon salt

Vegetable oil cooking spray for greasing

icing

1 cup (4 oz/125 g) confectioners' (icing) sugar

¼ teaspoon vanilla extract (essence)

4–5 teaspoons whole (full-cream) milk

● In a bowl, combine the butter, brown sugar, and molasses. Using an electric mixer on medium speed, beat until light and fluffy, about 3 minutes. Add the egg yolks and beat until incorporated.

● Sift together the flour, cinnamon, ginger, allspice, baking soda, cloves, and salt into a bowl. Add the flour mixture to the butter mixture and mix on low speed just until incorporated. Divide the dough into thirds, shape into flat disks, and wrap in plastic wrap. Refrigerate overnight.

● Position the oven rack in the upper third of the oven and preheat to 375°F (190°C). Grease 2 large, heavy cookie sheets with cooking spray.

● On a lightly floured surface, roll out 1 dough disk to ¼ inch (6 mm) thickness. Using cookie cutters that are about 5 inches (12½ cm) tall, cut out gingerbread people shapes. Using a metal spatula, transfer the shapes to a prepared cookie sheet, spacing them about 1 inch (2½ cm) apart. Gather the scraps into a ball, wrap in plastic wrap, and refrigerate. Repeat rolling and cutting with the remaining dough disks, one at a time.

● Bake until the cookies begin to turn golden brown on the edges, about 10 minutes. Transfer to wire racks and let cool completely.

● To make the icing, in a small bowl, combine the confectioners' sugar and vanilla. Stir in enough milk to thin to the desired consistency. Decorate the cookies with the icing. Let the icing dry completely before storing cookies in an airtight container at room temperature for up to 1 week.

makes about 40 cookies

cookie dough

$\frac{1}{2}$ cup (4 oz/125 g) unsalted butter, at room temperature

$\frac{3}{4}$ cup (6 oz/125 g) sugar

1 large egg

1$\frac{1}{2}$ teaspoons vanilla extract (essence)

1$\frac{1}{2}$ cups (7$\frac{1}{2}$ oz/235 g) all-purpose (plain) flour

1 teaspoon baking powder

$\frac{1}{4}$ teaspoon salt

Vegetable oil cooking spray for greasing

icing

4 cups (16 oz/500 g) confectioners' (icing) sugar, plus more as needed

$\frac{1}{4}$ cup (2 oz/60 g) unsalted butter, melted

2 teaspoons vanilla extract (essence)

$\frac{1}{4}$ cup (2 fl oz/60 ml) heavy (double) cream, or milk, plus more as needed

Food coloring, optional

Colored sugars and dragées for decorating, optional

iced sugar
cookies

• Using an electric mixer on medium-high speed, beat the butter and sugar until light and fluffy. Add the egg and vanilla and beat until incorporated.

• In another bowl, combine the flour, baking powder, and salt. Gradually add the flour mixture to the butter mixture and mix on low speed until incorporated. Divide the dough in half. Wrap each half in plastic wrap and refrigerate until firm, about 1 hour.

• Preheat the oven to 350°F (180°C). Lightly grease 2 cookie sheets with cooking spray. Roll out one dough half on a floured work surface until dough is $\frac{1}{8}$ inch (3 mm) thick.

• Using cookie cutters, cut out as many shapes as you can from the rolled dough. Using a metal spatula, transfer the shapes to the cookie sheets, spacing them about $\frac{1}{2}$ inch (12 mm) apart. Set the dough scraps aside. Roll out and cut shapes from the second dough half and transfer to sheets.

Gather all the dough scraps together, roll out, cut shapes, and place on sheets. Bake until light golden brown around the edges, 10–12 minutes. Transfer to wire racks to cool completely.

• To make the icing, sift the confectioners' sugar into a bowl. Add the melted butter, vanilla, and cream. Using an electric mixer on medium speed, beat until the mixture is smooth and creamy. If the icing seems too thin, add more confectioners' sugar; if it seems too thick, add a drop or two of cream. If you prefer different colors of icing, divide it among small bowls, then add 1 or 2 drops of desired food coloring to each bowl and stir well to blend.

• Using a small icing spatula, spread a thin layer of icing onto each cookie. If desired, use a small pastry bag fitted with a narrow writing tip to pipe raised decorations. Sprinkle the cookies with colored sugars or dragées, if desired. Set the cookies aside until the icing is completely dry.

nut crescent
cookies

makes about 24 cookies

1 cup (5 oz/155 g)
all-purpose (plain) flour

¾ cup (3 oz/90 g) walnuts

½ cup (4 oz/125 g) chilled
unsalted butter, cut into
pieces

¼ cup (2 oz/60 g) sugar

1 teaspoon vanilla extract
(essence)

½ teaspoon ground nutmeg

1 pinch salt

Confectioners' (icing) sugar
for dusting

● Preheat the oven to 325°F (165°C). Have ready an ungreased cookie sheet.

● In a food processor, combine the flour, walnuts, butter, sugar, vanilla, nutmeg, and salt. Pulse until the mixture resembles coarse meal, then process just until the dough begins to pull together.

● Pinch off about 2 teaspoons of the dough and roll it between your palms into a rope about 2½ inches (6 cm) long, slightly tapering it at both ends. Arrange the rope in a crescent shape on the baking sheet. Repeat with the remaining dough, spacing the ropes about 1 inch (2½ cm) apart on the cookie sheet.

● Bake until the cookies are just firm to the touch, about 20 minutes. Transfer the baking sheet to a wire rack and let the cookies cool for about 5 minutes. Then, using a small metal spatula, transfer the cookies to the wire rack to cool completely.

● Using a fine-mesh sieve, dust the cooled cookies with confectioners' sugar. Store in an airtight container at room temperature for up to 5 days.

brown sugar–
walnut rounds

makes about 36 cookies

1 cup (4 oz/125 g) walnuts, plus about 36 walnut halves for decorating

$^3/_4$ cup (6 oz/185 g) golden brown sugar, firmly packed

1 cup (8 oz/250 g) unsalted butter, at room temperature

$1^1/_2$ teaspoons maple extract (essence)

$^1/_4$ teaspoon salt

2 cups (10 oz/315 g) all-purpose (plain) flour

• Preheat the oven to 250°F (120°C). Have ready 2 ungreased cookie sheets.

• In a food processor, process the 1 cup (4 oz/125 g) walnuts until coarsely chopped; take care not to overprocess them. Add $^1/_4$ cup ($2^1/_2$ oz/75 g) of the brown sugar and process until the nuts are finely chopped; set aside.

• Combine the butter, the remaining $^1/_2$ cup ($3^1/_2$ oz/105 g) brown sugar, the maple extract, and the salt in a large bowl. Using an electric mixer on high speed, beat until light and fluffy. Add the flour and the nut mixture to the butter mixture and mix on low speed until just incorporated.

• Scoop up spoonfuls of the dough, then roll them into 1-inch ($2^1/_2$-cm) balls. Arrange the balls on the cookie sheets, spacing them $1^1/_2$ inches (4 cm) apart. Press a walnut half into the center of each ball.

• Bake until the cookies are brown around the edges, about 20 minutes. Using a metal spatula, transfer the cookies to wire racks to cool. Store in an airtight container at room temperature for up to 5 days.

vanilla bean
refrigerator cookies

makes about 42 cookies

vanilla sugar

1½ vanilla beans, cut into 1½-inch (4-cm) pieces

2 cups (16 oz/500 g) sugar

cookie dough

½ cup (4 oz/125 g) unsalted butter, at room temperature

1 large egg

1¾ cups (7 oz/220 g) sifted all-purpose (plain) flour

1½ teaspoons baking powder

⅛ teaspoon salt

Vegetable oil cooking spray for greasing

● In a food processor or blender, process the vanilla bean pieces and ½ cup (4 oz/125 g) of the sugar until the vanilla beans are finely chopped. Add the remaining 1½ cups (12 oz/375 g) of sugar and process until thoroughly incorporated. Pass the vanilla sugar through a fine-mesh sieve and discard any large pieces of vanilla bean.

● In a large bowl and using an electric mixer on high speed, beat the butter until light and fluffy. Add 1 cup (8 oz/250 g) of the vanilla sugar and beat until blended. Add the egg and beat until light and fluffy.

● In a bowl, sift together the flour, baking powder, and salt. Gradually add to the butter mixture and mix on low speed just until blended.

● Spoon the dough in a rough log 10 inches (25 cm) long down the center of a large sheet of waxed paper. Fold 1 side of the paper over the dough and, pressing with your hands, shape the dough into an even cylinder about 10 inches (25 cm) long. Wrap the log tightly in the waxed paper and refrigerate until firm, at least 4 hours and up to overnight.

● Preheat the oven to 400°F (200°C). Grease 2 cookie sheets with cooking spray. Unwrap and cut the chilled dough into slices ½ inch (12 mm) thick. Place the rounds on the cookie sheets 1 inch (2½ cm) apart and sprinkle evenly with ⅓ cup (2⅔ oz/85 g) of the vanilla sugar (reserve the remaining vanilla sugar for another use). Bake until the edges of the cookies are golden brown, about 12 minutes. Cool the cookies on wire racks. Store in an airtight container for up to 5 days.

spiced palmier
cookies

makes about 18 cookies

$\frac{1}{3}$ cup (3 oz/90 g) sugar

$\frac{1}{2}$ teaspoon ground cardamom

1 sheet, about 9 oz (280 g) frozen puff pastry, thawed

Vegetable oil cooking spray for greasing

• In a small bowl, stir together the sugar and cardamom. Sprinkle a work surface with about 1 tablespoon of the cardamom-sugar mixture. Open the puff pastry sheet and place it on top of the sugar mixture, and, using a rolling pin, roll it out into a rectangle about 9 by 11 inches (23 by 28 cm) and $\frac{1}{8}$ inch (3 mm) thick. Cut the pastry lengthwise into three equal strips, each about 3 inches (7$\frac{1}{2}$ cm) wide.

• Sprinkle each pastry strip evenly with 1 tablespoon of the remaining cardamom-sugar mixture. Working with 1 pastry strip, gently fold both ends inward so they meet in the center. Then bring both sides in to meet at the center, like closing a book; take care not to compress the pastry. Coat the outside with more of the cardamom-sugar mixture. Repeat to shape and coat the 2 remaining pastry strips, then refrigerate the strips for about 30 minutes.

• Meanwhile, preheat the oven to 350°F (180°C). Grease 2 cookie sheets with cooking spray.

• Using a sharp knife, cut the pastry strips crosswise into slices $\frac{1}{2}$ inch (12 mm) thick. Arrange the slices on the prepared cookie sheets, loosening the coil of each palmier slightly and spacing them about 2 inches (5 cm) apart on the sheets.

• Bake until the palmier bottoms turn golden brown, about 20 minutes. Use a metal spatula to turn over the palmiers and continue to bake until the tops are dark golden brown, about 5 minutes longer. Cool the cookies on wire racks. Store in an airtight container at room temperature for up to 5 days.

orange-oatmeal lace
cookies

• Preheat the oven to 350°F (180°C). Line 2 cookie sheets with parchment (baking) paper.

• In a bowl, combine the sugar, oats, flour, and baking powder and mix together with a wooden spoon. Add the melted butter, milk, molasses, orange zest, and vanilla and stir until just blended. Let the batter stand for 15 minutes.

• Using a tablespoon to shape the dough uniformly, drop the batter onto the prepared cookie sheets into mounds about 1 inch (2$\frac{1}{2}$ cm) in diameter, spacing the mounds about 3 inches (7$\frac{1}{2}$ cm) apart.

• Bake until the cookies are brown on the edges, about 10 minutes. Transfer the parchment paper with the cookies to a wire rack and let cool completely. Gently peel the cookies from the paper.

• To make the chocolate coating, combine the chocolate and shortening in a heatproof bowl. Place the bowl over a pan of simmering water, taking care that the bowl does not touch the water. Heat the mixture, stirring occasionally, just until the chocolate is melted and the mixture is smooth. Remove from the heat.

• Line 2 cookie sheets with waxed paper. Dip each cooled cookie in the chocolate coating, then place on the lined cookie sheets. Refrigerate until the chocolate sets, about 20 minutes. Gently remove the cookies from the paper. Store in an airtight container in the refrigerator for up to 5 days.

makes 48 cookies

cookie dough

¾ cup (6 oz/185 g) sugar

¾ cup (2¼ oz/70 g) quick-cooking oats, firmly packed

¾ cup (4 oz/125 g) all-purpose (plain) flour

½ teaspoon baking powder

½ cup (4 oz/125 g) unsalted butter, plus 2 tablespoons, melted

¼ cup (2 fl oz/60 ml) whole (full-cream) milk

¼ cup (3 oz/85 g) unsulfured light molasses

1 tablespoon orange zest, grated

1 teaspoon vanilla extract (essence)

chocolate coating

8 oz (250 g) semisweet (plain) or bittersweet chocolate, chopped

2 teaspoons trans-fat-free vegetable shortening (vegetable lard)

pecan
wafers

makes about 24 cookies

Vegetable oil cooking spray for greasing

½ cup (2 oz/60 g) **pecan pieces**

½ cup (4 oz/125 g) **sugar**

¼ cup (1½ oz/45 g) **all-purpose (plain) flour**

5 tablespoons **unsalted butter, melted and cooled**

2 large **egg whites, lightly beaten**

½ teaspoon **vanilla extract (essence)**

⅓ cup (1⅓ oz/40 g) **finely chopped pecans**

● Preheat the oven to 350°F (180°C). Grease a large, heavy cookie sheet with cooking spray. Have ready a dowel-shaped rolling pin.

● In a food processor, combine the pecan pieces and sugar and process until finely ground. Transfer to a bowl and stir in the flour with a rubber spatula. Add the melted butter, egg whites, and vanilla, and mix well.

● Working in batches, drop the batter by heaping teaspoonfuls onto the prepared cookie sheet, spacing the mounds at least 3 inches (7½ cm) apart. Using an icing spatula or a knife, spread each mound into a round about 2½ inches (6 cm) in diameter. Sprinkle each round with about ½ teaspoon of the chopped pecans. Bake until the edges of the cookies are dark golden and the centers are lightly golden, about 9 minutes.

● While the cookies are still very hot, and working quickly, use a thin metal spatula to lift each cookie from the baking sheet and drape it over the rolling pin. Let cool completely, then transfer the cookies to wire racks to cool. If the cookies cool too much and become too brittle to form, return the baking sheet to the oven briefly to soften them and continue shaping.

● Repeat to shape and bake the remaining cookies, greasing the baking sheet before portioning each batch. Store the cookies in an airtight container in the refrigerator for up to 2 weeks.

honey-orange
madeleines

makes 12 madeleines

5 tablespoons unsalted butter, at room temperature, plus melted butter for greasing

Scant $\frac{1}{3}$ cup ($2\frac{1}{3}$ oz/75 g) superfine (castor) sugar

2 teaspoons golden brown sugar

1 pinch salt

1 tablespoon honey

2 large eggs

$\frac{1}{2}$ cup ($2\frac{1}{2}$ oz/75 g) all-purpose (plain) flour, plus 2 tablespoons, plus extra for dusting

Scant 1 teaspoon baking powder

1 teaspoon grated orange zest

Confectioners' (icing) sugar, optional

● Preheat the oven to 350°F (180°C). Have ready a standard 12-mold madeleine pan.

● Add the 5 tablespoons butter to a large bowl. Using a wooden spoon, beat the butter until light and creamy. Add the superfine and brown sugars and mix well, then mix in the salt and honey. Add the eggs one at a time, beating well after each addition.

● In another bowl, sift together the $\frac{1}{2}$ cup ($2\frac{1}{2}$ oz/75 g) plus 2 tablespoons flour and the baking powder. Add the flour mixture and orange zest to the butter mixture and mix well.

● Use a pastry brush to coat the madeleine molds with the melted butter, then place the pan in the refrigerator until the butter hardens, about 2 minutes. Brush the molds again with the melted butter, then lightly dust them with flour, tapping out the excess.

● Spoon the batter evenly into the prepared molds, taking care not to overfill the molds. Bake until the madeleines are golden, 8–9 minutes. Cool the madeleines in the pan for a few seconds, then invert the pan and tap it onto a work surface to release the madeleines. Transfer the madeleines to wire racks to cool. If desired, dust with confectioners' sugar just before serving.

makes 48 cookies

cookie dough

1 cup (8 oz/250 g) unsalted butter, at room temperature, plus ¼ cup (2 oz/60 g) unsalted butter, melted and cooled

½ lb (8 oz/250 g) cream cheese, at room temperature

¼ teaspoon salt

2 cups (10 oz/315 g) all-purpose (plain) flour

Vegetable oil cooking spray for greasing

⅓ cup (2½ oz/75 g) golden brown sugar, firmly packed

⅓ cup (3 oz/90 g) sugar

2 teaspoons ground cinnamon

1½ cups (7½ oz/225 g) hazelnuts (filberts), toasted (see page 84), cooled, and finely chopped

topping

¼ cup (2 oz/60 g) sugar

¾ teaspoon ground cinnamon

1 egg white

cinnamon hazelnut
rugelach

● Combine the 1 cup (8 oz/250 g) room-temperature butter and cream cheese in a large bowl. Using an electric mixer on high speed, beat until the mixture is smooth. Add the salt and mix well. Add the flour and mix on low speed just until incorporated.

● On a floured work surface, using floured hands, shape the dough into a rough log and cut it into 4 equal pieces. Flatten each piece into a disk and wrap each disk in plastic wrap. Refrigerate until firm, at least 2 hours or up to overnight.

● Preheat the oven to 375°F (190°C). Grease 2 cookie sheets with cooking spray. In a small bowl, combine the brown sugar, $\frac{1}{3}$ cup (3 oz/90 g) sugar, and cinnamon.

● Let 1 dough disk stand at room temperature until slightly softened, about 10 minutes. Lightly flour the dough disk and place it between 2 sheets of waxed paper. Roll out the dough into a round $\frac{1}{8}$ inch (3 mm) thick and 10 inches (25 cm) in diameter. Remove the top sheet of waxed paper. Brush the dough with some of the melted butter,

then sprinkle with 3 tablespoons of the brown sugar mixture. Top with one-fourth of the chopped nuts. Using a rolling pin, gently press the filling to help it adhere to the dough round. Cut the round into quarters, then cut each quarter into 3 equal wedges to make 12 wedges total. Starting at the wide end, roll up each wedge to the point and transfer to a prepared cookie sheet, arranging the rolls point-side down and spacing them 1 inch (2.5 cm) apart.

● To make the topping, in a bowl, mix $\frac{1}{4}$ cup (2 oz/60 g) sugar and the cinnamon. In a small bowl, mix the egg white with 1 tablespoon water. Brush the cookies with the egg white–water mixture, then sprinkle with the cinnamon-sugar mixture.

● Bake until the cookies are golden brown, about 20 minutes. Transfer to wire racks to cool. Repeat to shape, fill, glaze, and bake the remaining dough disks. Store the baked rugelach in an airtight container at room temperature for up to 5 days.

anise biscotti
with walnuts & raisins

makes about 24 biscotti

½ cup (3 oz/90 g) raisins (sultanas)

1½ cups (6 oz/185 g) walnut pieces

½ cup (4 oz/125 g) unsalted butter, at room temperature

1 cup (8 oz/250 g) sugar

2 large eggs

1 tablespoon brandy

2 teaspoons vanilla extract (essence)

2 cups (10 oz/315 g) all-purpose (plain) flour

1 tablespoon aniseed

1½ teaspoons baking powder

¼ teaspoon salt

● In a bowl, stir together the raisins and ½ cup (4 fl oz/125 ml) warm water and let stand until soft, about 1 hour. Drain and set aside.

● Preheat the oven to 325°F (165°C). Spread the walnuts on a rimmed baking sheet and toast in the oven until fragrant and lightly colored, about 25 minutes. Let the nuts cool, then chop them coarsely. Leave the oven on. Line a large, heavy cookie sheet with parchment (baking) paper.

● In a large bowl, combine the butter and sugar. Using an electric mixer on medium speed, beat the mixture until light and fluffy, about 3 minutes. Add the eggs one at a time. Add the brandy and vanilla and mix well.

● In a bowl, stir together the flour, aniseed, baking powder, and salt. Gradually add the flour mixture to the butter mixture and mix on low speed just until incorporated. Add the walnuts and raisins and mix until just incorporated. With well-floured hands, divide the dough into 3 equal portions, evenly space them on the prepared cookie sheet, and shape each portion into a log about 14 inches (35 cm) long and 1½ inches (4 cm) in diameter. Bake until the logs feel firm to the touch and are lightly colored, about 40 minutes. Remove the logs from the oven and let cool on the sheet on a wire rack for 15 minutes. Leave the oven on.

● On a cutting board, cut each log on the diagonal into slices ⅜ inch (1 cm) wide using a serrated knife. Transfer the slices to unlined cookie sheets, cut sides down. Bake until lightly golden and dry, 15–20 minutes. Cool on wire racks. Store in an airtight container for up to 1 week.

hazelnut almond
cookies

makes 36 cookies

1¼ cups (6¼ oz/190 g) hazelnuts (filberts)

¾ cup (3 oz/95 g) confectioners' (icing) sugar, plus 3 tablespoons

1 teaspoon all-purpose (plain) flour

2 egg whites

⅓ cup (3 oz/90 g) sugar

¾ teaspoon almond extract (essence)

● Preheat the oven to 300°F (150°C). Line a large, heavy cookie sheet with parchment (baking) paper.

● In a food processor, process the hazelnuts until finely ground; take care not to overprocess them into a paste. Add ¼ cup (1 oz/30 g) of the confectioners' sugar and process to a powder. Add the remaining ½ cup (2 oz/65 g) plus 3 tablespoons confectioners' sugar and the flour and process until just incorporated.

● To an impeccably clean and dry bowl, add the egg whites and bring them to room temperature. Using an electric mixer with clean beaters on medium speed, beat the egg whites until soft peaks form. Increase the speed, gradually add the sugar, and beat until stiff, shiny peaks form. Using a rubber spatula, fold in the almond extract and the hazelnut mixture.

● Fit a pastry bag with a ½-inch (12-mm) plain tip. Spoon the batter into the bag and twist to seal the end. Pipe the batter onto the prepared cookie sheet in mounds about 1½ inches (4 cm) in diameter, spacing them 1 inch (2½ cm) apart. Using a wet finger, smooth the top of each mound.

● Bake until the cookies are just beginning to brown, about 45 minutes. Turn off the oven, leave the oven door closed, and let the cookies stand for 30 minutes to dry in the residual heat of the oven.

● Use a metal spatula to transfer the cookies to wire racks to cool. Store in an airtight container at room temperature for up to 1 month.

chocolate-filled
kisses

• In a large bowl, combine the 1 cup (8 oz/ 250 g) butter, confectioners' sugar, and salt. Using an electric mixer on medium speed, beat until light and fluffy. Add the rum and beat until incorporated. Add the flour and beat on low speed just until smooth and well blended. Cover the bowl and refrigerate the dough until firm, about 1 hour.

• Preheat the oven to 350°F (180°C). Have ready 2 ungreased cookie sheets.

• Scoop up teaspoonfuls of the dough and then roll each spoonful between your palms into a ball. Place the balls about 1 inch (2½ cm) apart on the cookie sheets. Bake until the cookies are firm but not browned, 10–12 minutes. Transfer the cookies to wire racks to cool completely.

• Place the chocolate and the remaining 2 tablespoons butter in a heatproof bowl. Place the bowl over (not touching) a pan of simmering water and heat, stirring occasionally, until the chocolate and butter melt and the mixture is smooth. Remove the bowl from the pan and let cool slightly.

• Using a table knife, spread a small amount of the chocolate mixture on the bottom of a cookie. Place the bottom of a second cookie against the chocolate, lining up the edges sandwich style, and press the halves together. Repeat to make the sandwiches with the remaining cookies and chocolate. Let cool on the wire racks until the filling is set. Store in an airtight container in a cool place for up to 1 week.

makes 24 cookies

1 cup (8 oz/250 g) unsalted
butter, plus 2 tablespoons
at room temperature

$\frac{1}{2}$ cup ($2\frac{1}{2}$ oz/75 g)
confectioners' (icing) sugar

$\frac{1}{2}$ teaspoon salt

1 tablespoon rum

2 cups (10 oz/305 g)
all-purpose (plain) flour

2 oz (60 g) high-quality
semisweet (plain) chocolate

mint chocolate
cookies

makes about 48 cookies

¾ cup (6 oz/185 g) unsalted butter, at room temperature

¾ cup (6 oz/185 g) sugar

1 large egg

1½ teaspoons vanilla extract (essence)

1½ teaspoons peppermint extract (essence)

⅛ teaspoon salt

¼ cup (¾ oz/20 g) unsweetened cocoa powder, preferably Dutch-process

1½ cups (7½ oz/235 g) all-purpose (plain) flour

● Preheat the oven to 375°F (190°C). Have ready 2 ungreased cookie sheets and a cookie press with design plates.

● In a large bowl, combine the butter and sugar. Using an electric mixer on high speed, beat until light and fluffy. Add the egg, vanilla and peppermint, and salt, and beat until incorporated. Reduce the speed to low, add the cocoa powder, and mix well. Add the flour and mix until well blended.

● Following the manufacturer's instructions, fit the cookie press with the desired design plate, then fill the cookie press with the dough. Press the dough directly onto the cookie sheets, spacing the cookies about 1 inch (2½ cm) apart.

● Bake until the cookies are firm to the touch, about 10 minutes. Transfer the cookies to wire racks to cool. Store in an airtight container for up to 5 days.

almond
meringues

makes about 30 meringues

$\frac{1}{2}$ cup (2$\frac{1}{2}$ oz/75 g) slivered blanched almonds

3 large egg whites, at room temperature

$\frac{1}{2}$ cup (4 oz/125 g) sugar

● Preheat the oven to 350°F (180°C). Spread the almonds on a rimmed baking sheet and toast in the oven, stirring occasionally, until lightly browned and fragrant, about 8 minutes. Immediately transfer to a plate to cool completely, then chop finely.

● Reduce the oven temperature to 200°F (95°C). Line 2 cookie sheets with aluminum foil or parchment (baking) paper.

● To an impeccably clean and dry, large bowl, add the egg whites. Using an electric mixer with clean beaters on high speed, beat the egg whites until soft peaks form. Gradually add the sugar, beating until glossy, firm peaks form. Using a rubber spatula, gently fold in the almonds, taking care not to deflate the mixture too much.

● Fit a pastry bag with a $\frac{1}{2}$-inch (12-mm) star. Spoon the egg white mixture into the bag, then pipe it in mounds about 1$\frac{1}{2}$ inches (4 cm) in diameter onto the prepared cookie sheets. Space the mounds about 1$\frac{1}{2}$ inches (4 cm) apart.

● Bake until the meringues are crisp and dry, about 2 hours. Remove from the oven and use a sharp knife to loosen the bottoms of the meringues from the foil or paper. Let the meringues cool completely on the baking sheets. Store in an airtight container at room temperature for up to 5 days.

makes about 36 cookies

1 cup (8 oz/250 g) unsalted butter, at room temperature

1 cup (8 oz/250 g) sugar

1 large egg

2$\frac{1}{2}$ teaspoons vanilla extract (essence)

$\frac{1}{2}$ teaspoon ground cardamom

$\frac{1}{2}$ teaspoon salt

2$\frac{1}{2}$ cups (12$\frac{1}{2}$ oz/390 g) sifted all-purpose (plain) flour

Confectioners' (icing) sugar for sprinkling

vanilla-cardamom
wafers

- Preheat the oven to 375°F (190°C). Have ready 2 ungreased cookie sheets and a cookie press with a ribbon design plate.

- In a large bowl, combine the butter and sugar. Using an electric mixer on high speed, beat the mixture until light and fluffy. Add the egg, vanilla, cardamom, and salt and beat until incorporated. Add the flour, then switch to a wooden spoon and stir until well blended.

- Following the manufacturer's instructions, fit the cookie press with the ribbon design plate and then fill the press with the dough. Press the dough out directly onto the cookie sheets in 4-inch (10-cm) strips.

- Bake until the cookies are golden brown, about 10 minutes. Use a metal spatula to gently transfer the cookies to wire racks to cool. Sprinkle the cooled cookies with confectioners' sugar. Store the cookies in an airtight container at room temperature for up to 4 days.

key lime
squares

- Preheat the oven to 350°F (180°C). Have ready a 9-by-13-by-2-inch (23-by-33-by-5-cm) baking pan.

- In a food processor, combine 2$\frac{1}{4}$ cups (11 oz/350 g) of the flour, the $\frac{1}{2}$ cup (2 oz/65 g) confectioners' sugar, the butter, the cream cheese, and the almond extract. Pulse just until the mixture is crumbly but holds together when squeezed between your fingers. Working quickly, transfer the dough to the pan and press it evenly into the bottom and $\frac{1}{2}$ inch (12 mm) up the sides of the pan to form the crust. Bake the crust until lightly browned, 20–25 minutes. Transfer the pan to a wire rack and let cool for 10 minutes. Leave the oven on.

- In a large bowl, combine the eggs, sugar, lime zest and juice, vanilla, and the remaining $\frac{1}{4}$ cup (1$\frac{1}{2}$ oz/40 g) flour. Use a whisk to mix until well blended. Pour the egg-lime mixture over the warm baked crust.

- Bake until the center is slightly soft, but set and no longer sticky, 22–24 minutes. Transfer to a wire rack and let cool completely. Cover and refrigerate for at least 6 hours or up to overnight.

- Just before serving, use a sharp knife to cut into 36 squares. Using a fine-mesh sieve, dust the tops with confectioners' sugar. Store in the refrigerator, dusting with additional confectioners' sugar just before serving.

makes 36 squares

2½ cups (12½ oz/390 g) all-purpose (plain) flour

½ cup (2 oz/65 g) confectioners' (icing) sugar, plus extra for dusting

½ cup (4 oz/125 g) chilled unsalted butter, cut into ½-inch cubes

3 oz (90 g) chilled cream cheese, cut into ½-inch (12-mm) cubes

¼ teaspoon almond extract (essence)

4 large eggs

2 cups (16 oz/500 g) sugar

1 tablespoon key lime zest, from about 4 limes

½ cup (4 fl oz/125 ml) fresh key lime juice, from 8–10 limes

1 teaspoon vanilla extract (essence)

triple chocolate mocha brownies

makes 16 brownies

¹⁄₂ cup (4 oz/125 g) unsalted butter, cut into pieces

4 oz (125 g) unsweetened chocolate, coarsely chopped

3 tablespoons instant espresso powder

2 cups (14 oz/440 g) golden brown sugar, firmly packed

4 large eggs

1 cup (5 oz/155 g) all-purpose (plain) flour

¹⁄₄ teaspoon salt

¹⁄₂ cup (2¹⁄₂ oz/75 g) macadamia nuts, chopped

3 oz (90 g) bittersweet chocolate, chopped

3 oz (90 g) white chocolate, chopped

• Preheat the oven to 375°F (190°C). Line an 8-by-8-by-2-inch (20-by-20-by-5-cm) baking pan with aluminum foil, letting the foil overhang the sides. Grease the foil.

• In a large, heavy saucepan, combine the butter, unsweetened chocolate, and espresso powder. Place the pan over low heat and stir frequently until the butter is melted and the mixture is smooth. Remove from the heat, add the brown sugar, and stir until smooth. Add the eggs one at a time and, using a wooden spoon, beat well after each addition. Add the flour and salt and beat until combined. Finally, add the nuts and the bittersweet and white chocolates and mix gently just until evenly distributed. Pour the batter into the prepared pan, using a rubber spatula to scrape any batter clinging to the bowl and to smooth the top.

• Bake until the brownie pulls away from the sides of the pan, about 40 minutes. Remove from the oven and let cool completely in the pan on a wire rack.

• To serve, remove the brownie from the pan by pulling up on the foil overhang and place on a cutting board. Use a large knife to cut the brownie into 16 bars. Wrap the brownies individually in plastic wrap and store at room temperature for up to 3 days.

white chocolate macadamia blondies

makes 24 blondies

½ cup (4 oz/125 g) unsalted butter, plus more for greasing, at room temperature

1¼ cups (9 oz/280 g) golden brown sugar, firmly packed

2 teaspoons instant espresso powder

1 teaspoon vanilla extract (essence)

2 large eggs

1 cup (5 oz/155 g) all-purpose (plain) flour

¾ cup (3¾ oz/115 g) macadamia nuts, coarsely chopped

3–4 oz (90–125 g) white chocolate, coarsely chopped

Caramel Glaze, page 76

● Preheat the oven to 350°F (180°C). Line an 8-by-8-by-2-inch (20-by-20-by-5-cm) baking pan with aluminum foil, letting the foil overhang the sides. Grease the foil with butter.

● In a large bowl, combine the butter, brown sugar, espresso powder, and vanilla. Using an electric mixer on high speed, beat the mixture until light and fluffy. Add the eggs one at a time, beating well after each addition. Continue to beat until very fluffy, about 2 minutes. Reduce the speed to low, add the flour, and mix until incorporated. Add the nuts and chocolate and mix on low speed just until blended. Pour the batter into the prepared pan, using a rubber spatula to scrape any batter clinging to the bowl and to smooth the top.

● Bake until a toothpick inserted in the center comes out clean, about 40 minutes. Let cool in the pan on a wire rack.

● Drizzle the blondie with Caramel Glaze. Cut the blondie into 24 bars. Wrap the blondies individually in plastic wrap and store at room temperature for up to 3 days.

muffins

Muffins earn the adjective "perfect" for so many good reasons.

First comes the speed with which you can make them. Like all batter-based breads leavened with baking powder, muffins can be assembled in minutes and baked almost as quickly. Next, there's the variety. A swiftly mixed muffin batter lends itself to all kinds of embellishments, from fruit to nuts to chocolate, not to mention savory additions like cheeses, herbs, and spices. Muffins also win admirers for how well they suit any kind of meal, from breakfast and brunch to lunch and dinner to snack time. Finally, there's the simple pleasure of eating any sort of fresh-baked muffin, warm and bursting with flavor.

Whatever kind of muffin you might prepare, this book makes perfection easy with more than two dozen different kitchen-tested recipes. You'll find standard muffins made in a pan with a ½-cup (4-fl oz/125-ml) capacity; large muffins made in a pan with a 1-cup (8-fl oz/250-ml) capacity; and mini muffins baked in a pan with a ¼-cup (2-fl oz/60-ml) capacity. And, along with the added support of the tips on the following pages, each recipe provides all the instructions you need to achieve perfection.

So start baking, and enjoy your own definition of the perfect muffin!

muffin basics

Being so-called quick breads, mixed with a few stirs and leavened simply by baking powder, muffins don't demand much in the way of baking expertise. But some basic knowledge will nonetheless help ensure that you get perfect muffins every time.

● **Read and follow the recipe.** Before you begin, review the ingredients and instructions. Follow all instructions faithfully to achieve the desired results.

● **Use the right equipment.** Each of the recipes in this book assumes you have its specified size of metal muffin pan; such pans require either greasing with nonstick baking spray, butter, or shortening, or lining with parchment (baking) paper liners. You can also use one of today's popular nonstick flexible silicone muffin pans, placed on a rigid baking sheet before filling to make it easier to put into and take out of the oven.

● **Prep ingredients in advance and measure precisely.** Before you start making any muffin recipe, read its ingredients list for specifics on how to measure and prepare each item. Have dry and liquid measuring cups on hand and use accordingly. Line up all of the ingredients in your work area, ready to use at the right moment.

● **Don't overstir.** When preparing any muffin batter, note the standard instruction to stir just until the ingredients are moistened but still lumpy. Overstirring can result in tough muffins.

● **Enjoy yourself.** Making muffins should always be a pleasure, just another reason they're so perfect.

makes 12 standard
muffins

1 cup (5 oz/155 g)
processed wheat bran

1 cup (8 fl oz/250 ml)
skim milk

$\frac{1}{2}$ cup (4 oz/125 g)
unsalted butter,
at room temperature

1 cup (7 oz/220 g) lightly
packed light brown sugar

1 egg

2 cups (10 oz/315 g)
whole-wheat (wholemeal)
self-rising flour

1 teaspoon baking powder

1 cup (4 oz/125 g) fresh or
frozen blueberries

whole-grain blueberry
bran muffins

Whole-wheat (wholemeal) flour makes this variation on a morning classic extra nourishing. Try it with fresh or frozen raspberries.

● Preheat the oven to 400°F (200°C). Grease 12 standard (½-cup/125-ml) muffin cups or line them with parchment (baking) paper liners.

● Put the bran and milk in a bowl and leave at room temperature until all of the liquid is absorbed, about 30 minutes.

● In a mixing bowl, using a hand-held electric mixer on high speed, cream together the butter and sugar until light and fluffy. Beat in the egg. Add the bran mixture. Sift together the flour and baking powder, then fold them into the butter-and-sugar mixture, mixing well. Stir in the blueberries just until evenly distributed.

● Spoon the batter into the prepared muffin cups, filling them two-thirds full. Bake until the muffins are golden brown and a wooden skewer or toothpick inserted into the center of one comes out clean, 15–20 minutes. Remove the muffins from the oven and cool in the pan for 5 minutes. Serve warm, or transfer the muffins to a wire rack to cool.

glazed maple and banana
microwave muffins

This recipe assumes a 650-watt microwave oven; if yours has a different wattage, adjust the cooking time accordingly.

makes 6 large muffins

muffins

2 eggs

⅓ cup (2½ oz/75 g) firmly packed light brown sugar

⅓ cup (3 oz/90 g) unsalted butter, cubed

2 small ripe bananas, cut into chunks

⅓ cup (3 fl oz/90 ml) pure maple syrup

¼ teaspoon baking soda (bicarbonate of soda)

1½ cups (7½ oz/235 g) self-rising flour

glaze

1 cup (4 oz/125 g) confectioners' (icing) sugar

1 teaspoon unsweetened cocoa powder

¼ cup (2 fl oz/60 ml) pure maple syrup

1–2 teaspoons water

Chopped walnuts (optional)

● For the muffins, put the eggs and brown sugar in a food processor with a stainless-steel blade. Process for 1 minute. With the motor running, drop the butter cubes and the banana pieces through the feed tube and process until completely smooth. With the motor still running, add the syrup and baking soda; then, add the flour in one pour and stop processing. Scrape down the sides with a rubber spatula. Return the lid to the processor and pulse once or twice more to complete mixing.

● Pour the batter into 6 large (1-cup/250-ml) microwave-safe muffin cups. Elevate the cups from the oven floor, arranging them 3 at a time around the perimeter of the turntable. Cook on the high setting (100 percent power) until well risen and spongy, about 4 minutes. Leave in their cups for 5 minutes, loosely covered; then, transfer to a wire rack to cool completely. Cook the remaining batter in the same way.

● For the glaze, clean out and dry the work bowl and blade. Put the confectioners' sugar and cocoa in the work bowl with the blade and process until mixed. With the motor running, gradually pour the syrup through the feed tube, stopping when the glaze is fluid. If necessary, pulse in a little water for a more fluid consistency.

● Using a tablespoon, spoon the glaze over the cooled muffins, letting it flow down the sides. Decorate with chopped walnuts if desired.

oat muffins
with bananas and golden raisins

Packed with flavor and goodness, these are great for breakfast. Use very ripe bananas, with skins splotched with black spots.

makes 6 large muffins

2 cups (10 oz/315 g) self-rising flour

1 teaspoon ground cinnamon

1/2 teaspoon baking soda (bicarbonate of soda)

1 cup (3 oz/90 g) rolled oats, plus 1/3 cup (1 oz/30 g) extra

1/2 cup (3 oz/90 g) golden raisins (sultanas)

1/2 cup (3 1/2 oz/105 g) firmly packed dark brown sugar

2 eggs, lightly beaten

3/4 cup (6 fl oz/180 ml) milk

1/4 cup (2 fl oz/60 ml) vegetable oil

2 very ripe medium bananas, mashed (to yield about 1 cup/ 8 oz/250 g)

1/2 cup (3 1/2 oz/110 g) Demerara sugar

● Preheat the oven to 400°F (200°C). Grease 6 large (1-cup/250-ml) muffin cups or line them with parchment (baking) paper liners.

● In a large mixing bowl, sift together the flour, cinnamon, and baking soda. Stir in the 1 cup (3 oz/90 g) of oats, the raisins, and the dark brown sugar. Make a well in the center.

● In a small mixing bowl, combine the eggs, milk, oil, and banana. Add all at once to the flour mixture and stir until just moistened (the batter should be lumpy).

● Spoon the batter into the prepared muffin cups, filling them two-thirds full. Sprinkle with the Demerara sugar and the extra rolled oats.

● Bake until the muffins are golden brown and a wooden skewer or toothpick inserted into the center of one comes out clean, 25–30 minutes. Remove the muffins from the oven and cool them in the pan for 5 minutes. Serve warm, or transfer to a wire rack to cool.

date and apple muffins
with coconut topping

Whether you use fresh dates, at their peak from mid-autumn through mid-winter, or dried dates, choose only plump, shiny specimens.

- Preheat the oven to 375°F (190°C). Grease 6 large (1-cup/250-ml) muffin cups or line them with parchment (baking) paper liners.

- For the muffins, in a mixing bowl, combine the apple, dates, baking soda, and boiling water. Set aside to cool to room temperature.

- In a mixing bowl, using a hand-held electric mixer on high speed, cream together the butter and sugar until light and fluffy. Beat in the egg. Fold in the sifted flour in several batches, alternating with the mixture of apple and dates.

- Spoon the batter into the prepared muffin cups, filling them two-thirds full. Bake them for 15 minutes, then remove the muffins from the oven and leave them to cool slightly while you make the topping. Leave the oven on.

- For the topping, put the butter, brown sugar, and coconut in a small saucepan and stir over moderate heat until the butter melts and the ingredients are combined.

- Spoon the topping over the muffins and return them to the oven. Bake until the topping is bubbling and golden and a wooden skewer or toothpick inserted into the center of a muffin comes out clean, 5–8 minutes more. Serve warm, or transfer to a wire rack to cool.

makes 6 large muffins

muffins

1 large green apple, peeled, cored, and finely chopped

1 cup (6 oz/185 g) chopped pitted dates

1 teaspoon baking soda (bicarbonate of soda)

1 cup (8 fl oz/250 ml) boiling water

½ cup (4 oz/125 g) unsalted butter

¾ cup (6 oz/185 g) granulated (white) sugar

1 egg, lightly beaten

2 cups (10 oz/315 g) self-rising flour, sifted

topping

¼ cup (2 oz/60 g) unsalted butter

½ cup (3½ oz/100 g) firmly packed light brown sugar

½ cup (1 oz/30 g) shredded coconut

sun-dried cherry
and walnut muffins

*Available in well-stocked food stores and specialty cooking shops,
sun-dried cherries are chewy and intensely flavored, like raisins.*

makes 12 standard muffins

2 cups (10 oz/315 g) self-rising
flour

½ teaspoon baking powder

⅓ teaspoon salt

⅓ cup (3 oz/90 g) sugar

½ teaspoon ground cinnamon

¼ teaspoon ground nutmeg

2 eggs, lightly beaten

1 cup (8 fl oz/250 ml) milk

¼ cup (2 oz/60 g) unsalted
butter, melted

1 tablespoon finely grated orange
zest

¾ cup (3 oz/90 g) pitted
sun-dried cherries

½ cup (2 oz/60 g) chopped
walnuts

● Preheat the oven to 400°F (200°C). Grease 12 standard (½-cup/125-ml) muffin cups or line them with parchment (baking) paper liners.

● In a medium mixing bowl, sift together the flour, baking powder, and salt. Stir in the sugar, cinnamon, and nutmeg. Make a well in the center.

● In a small mixing bowl, combine the eggs, milk, and melted butter. Add all at once to the flour mixture and stir until just moistened (the batter should be lumpy). Add the orange zest, sun-dried cherries, and walnuts. Stir briefly until just combined.

● Spoon the batter into the prepared muffin cups, filling them two-thirds full. Bake until the muffins are golden brown and a wooden skewer or toothpick inserted into the center of one comes out clean, 15–20 minutes. Remove the muffins from the oven and cool them in the pan for 5 minutes. Serve warm, or transfer to a wire rack to cool.

fresh pear muffins
with raisins

High in flavor but low in fat, these muffins are ideal for breakfast. Use a ripe but firm pear, so the pieces will hold their shape.

makes 12 standard muffins

2 cups (10 oz/315 g) self-rising flour

1 teaspoon ground nutmeg

½ cup (3½ oz/105 g) packed dark brown sugar

½ cup (3 oz/90 g) raisins, chopped

2 eggs, lightly beaten

1 cup (8 fl oz/250 ml) pear juice or apple juice

⅓ cup (3 fl oz/80 ml) vegetable oil

1 large pear, peeled, cored, and finely chopped

½ cup (2 oz/60 g) chopped walnuts

½ cup (4 oz/125 g) raw sugar

● Preheat the oven to 400°F (200°C). Grease 12 standard (½-cup/125-ml) muffin cups or line them with parchment (baking) paper liners.

● In a large mixing bowl, sift together the flour and nutmeg. Stir in the brown sugar and raisins. Make a well in the center.

● In a small mixing bowl, combine the eggs, juice, and oil. Add all at once to the flour mixture together with the chopped pear and stir until just moistened (the batter should be lumpy). Spoon the batter into the prepared muffin cups, filling them two-thirds full. Sprinkle the tops with the walnuts and raw sugar.

● Bake until the muffins are golden brown and a wooden skewer or toothpick inserted into the center of one comes out clean, 15–20 minutes. Remove the muffins from the oven and cool them in the pan for 5 minutes. Serve warm or transfer to a wire rack to cool.

makes 12 standard
muffins

2 cups (10 oz/315 g)
self-rising flour

½ teaspoon baking soda
(bicarbonate of soda)

½ cup (4 oz/125 g)
granulated (white) sugar

1 cup (6 oz/185 g)
semisweet (plain) chocolate
chips

2 eggs, lightly beaten

½ cup (4 fl oz/125 ml) milk

¼ cup (2 oz/60 g) unsalted
butter, melted

2 very ripe medium
bananas, mashed (to yield
about 1 cup/8 oz/250 g)

banana muffins
with chocolate chips

A perfect complement to chocolate, banana adds moisture, flavor, and golden color to these muffins. Use very ripe bananas for the best results.

• Preheat the oven to 400°F (200°C). Grease 12 standard (½-cup/125-ml) muffin cups or line them with parchment (baking) paper liners.

• In a large mixing bowl, sift together the self-rising flour and baking soda. Stir in the sugar and ½ cup (3 oz/90 g) of the chocolate chips. Make a well in the center.

• In a small mixing bowl, stir together the eggs, milk, melted butter, and mashed banana. Add all at once to the flour mixture and stir until just moistened (the batter should be lumpy).

• Spoon the batter into the prepared muffin cups, filling them two-thirds full. Sprinkle with the remaining ½ cup (3 oz/90 g) of chocolate chips.

• Bake until the muffins are golden brown and a wooden skewer or toothpick inserted into the center of one comes out clean, 15–20 minutes. Remove the muffins from the oven and cool in the pan for 5 minutes. Serve warm, or transfer to a wire rack to cool.

apricot and apple
muffins with almond topping

Chewy dried fruit combines with tangy orange in these tasty muffins. An almond-and-sugar topping adds appealing crunch.

- Preheat the oven to 400°F (200°C). Generously grease 12 standard (½-cup/125-ml) muffin cups or line them with parchment (baking) paper liners.

- In a small bowl, combine the chopped dried apricots and apple with the orange juice. Leave to soak at room temperature for 15 minutes.

- In a large mixing bowl, sift the flour. Stir in the brown sugar. Make a well in the center.

- In a small mixing bowl, combine the eggs, buttermilk, butter, and orange zest. Add all at once to the flour mixture, together with the soaked dried fruit and orange juice. Stir until just moistened (the batter should be lumpy).

- Spoon the batter into the prepared muffin cups, filling them two-thirds full. For the topping, scatter the slivered almonds and the Demerara sugar over the muffin batter.

- Bake until the muffins are golden brown and a wooden skewer or toothpick inserted into the center of one comes out clean, 15–20 minutes. Remove from the oven and cool in the pan for 5 minutes. Serve warm, or transfer the muffins to a wire rack to cool.

makes 12
standard muffins

muffins

½ cup (3 oz/90 g) chopped
dried apricots

½ cup (3 oz/90 g) chopped
dried apple

½ cup (4 fl oz/125 ml)
orange juice

2 cups (10 oz/315 g)
self-rising flour

½ cup (3½ oz/105 g) firmly
packed light brown sugar

2 eggs, lightly beaten

1 cup (8 fl oz/250 ml)
buttermilk

¼ cup (2 oz/60 g) unsalted
butter, melted

1 teaspoon grated orange
zest

topping

½ cup (2½ oz/75 g) slivered
almonds

⅓ cup (2½ oz/75 g)
Demerara sugar

makes 6 large muffins

2 cups (10 oz/315 g)
self-rising flour

½ cup (4 oz/125 g)
granulated (white) sugar

1 cup (4 oz/125 g)
chopped fresh strawberries

2 eggs, lightly beaten

1 cup (8 fl oz/250 ml) milk

¼ cup (2 oz/60 g) unsalted
butter, melted

¼ cup (2¾ oz/80 g)
strawberry jam, plus
1 tablespoon extra

1 teaspoon vanilla extract
(essence)

2 ounces (60 g) cream
cheese, cut into 6 cubes

confectioners' (icing) sugar,
for dusting

cheesecake muffins
with fresh strawberries

Along with a double dose of delicious strawberries, these jumbo muffins contain a hidden surprise: a cube of cream cheese in the center.

• Preheat the oven to 400°F (200°C). Grease 6 large (1-cup/250-ml) muffin cups or line them with parchment (baking) paper liners.

• In a large mixing bowl, sift the flour. Stir in the granulated sugar. With a paper towel, gently wipe the chopped strawberry pieces to soak up excess juice and prevent it from coloring the batter. Add the strawberry pieces to the dry ingredients. Make a well in the center.

• In a small mixing bowl, combine the eggs, milk, butter, ¼ cup (2¾ oz/80 g) jam, and vanilla. Add all at once to the flour mixture and stir until just moistened (the batter should be lumpy).

• Spoon two-thirds of the batter into the prepared muffin cups, distributing it evenly. Place a cube of cream cheese in the center of each cup and top with a little of the extra jam. Cover with the remaining batter.

• Bake until the muffins are golden brown and a wooden skewer or toothpick inserted into the cake part of one muffin comes out clean, 25–30 minutes. Remove from the oven and cool in the pan for 5 minutes. Serve warm, dusted with confectioners' sugar.

crumb-topped
cherry pie muffins

Use the same fruit you'd put into a pie for these muffins: tart red cherries that hold up well in baking.

makes 6 large or
12 standard muffins

crumb topping

¼ cup (2 oz/60 g) packed
dark brown sugar

2 tablespoons all-purpose (plain)
flour

2 tablespoons unsalted butter

muffins

1¾ cups (9 oz/280 g) all-purpose
(plain) flour

2 teaspoons baking powder

¼ teaspoon salt

¼ teaspoon ground nutmeg

⅓ cup (3 oz/90 g) granulated
(white) sugar

1 egg, beaten

¾ cup (6 fl oz/180 ml) milk

¼ cup (2 fl oz/60 ml) vegetable oil

1 cup (5 oz/155 g) pitted tart red
cherries (fresh, frozen, or drained
canned), coarsely chopped

● Preheat the oven to 400°F (200°C). Grease 6 large (1-cup/250-ml) or 12 standard (½-cup/125-ml) muffin cups or line them with parchment (baking) paper liners.

● For the crumb topping, in a small mixing bowl, combine the brown sugar and flour. With a pastry blender, two knives, or your fingertips, cut or rub in the butter until the mixture resembles coarse crumbs. Set aside.

● For the muffins, in a large mixing bowl, sift together the flour, baking powder, salt, and nutmeg. Stir in the granulated sugar. Make a well in the center.

● In a medium mixing bowl, combine the egg, milk, and oil. Add all at once to the flour mixture and stir until just moistened (the batter should be lumpy). Stir in the cherries.

● Spoon the batter into the prepared muffin cups, filling them two-thirds full. Sprinkle the topping over the muffins. Bake until the muffins are golden brown and a wooden skewer or toothpick inserted into the center of one comes out clean, about 25 minutes for large muffins or 20 minutes for standard muffins. Remove from the oven and cool in the pan for 5 minutes. Serve warm, or transfer to a wire rack to cool.

semolina and orange
mini muffins

Drizzled over the hot-from-the-oven muffins, an orange-flavored syrup makes these treats extra moist and delicious.

makes 24 mini muffins

muffins

2 cups (10 oz/315 g) self-rising flour

½ teaspoon baking powder

1 cup (4 oz/125 g) fine semolina

½ cup (4 oz/125 g) sugar

2 eggs, lightly beaten

1 cup (8 fl oz/250 ml) milk

¼ cup (2 oz/60 g) unsalted butter, melted

2 teaspoons grated orange zest

½ cup (4 fl oz/125 ml) orange juice

orange syrup

½ cup (4 oz/125 g) sugar

finely shredded zest of 1 small orange

½ cup (4 fl oz/125 ml) orange juice

½ cup (4 fl oz/125 ml) water

● Preheat the oven to 400°F (200°C). Grease 24 mini (¼-cup/60-ml) muffin cups or line them with parchment (baking) paper liners.

● In a large mixing bowl, sift together the flour and baking powder. Stir in the semolina and sugar. Make a well in the center.

● In a small mixing bowl, combine the eggs, milk, butter, orange zest, and juice. Add all at once to the flour mixture and stir until just moistened (the batter should be lumpy).

● Spoon the batter into the prepared muffin cups, filling them two-thirds full. Bake until golden brown and a wooden skewer or toothpick inserted into the center of one comes out clean, 12–15 minutes.

● Meanwhile, make the orange syrup: Put the sugar, orange zest, orange juice, and water in a small saucepan. Stir over low heat, without boiling, until the sugar has dissolved. Bring to a boil and simmer until syrupy and reduced by about one-third, about 10 minutes.

● Remove the muffins from the oven; do not remove them from their cups. While the muffins are still hot, prick them all over with a fine skewer. Pour the hot syrup over them. Set aside to cool a little and soak up the syrup before removing from the muffin cups. Serve warm, or transfer to a wire rack to cool.

poppy seed
and almond muffins

Make these almond-scented muffins bite-sized for a buffet. For breakfast or snacks, bake a batch of larger standard-sized ones.

- Preheat the oven to 400°F (200°C). Lightly grease 24 mini (¼-cup/60-ml) or 12 standard (½-cup/125-ml) muffin cups or line them with parchment (baking) paper liners.

- In a mixing bowl, sift together the flour, poppy seeds, baking powder, and salt. Stir in the ½ cup (4 oz/125 g) sugar. Make a well in the center.

- In a small mixing bowl, combine the egg, milk, oil, and almond extract. Add all at once to the flour mixture and stir until just moistened (the batter should be lumpy).

- Spoon the batter into the prepared muffin cups, filling them two-thirds full. Bake until the muffins are golden brown and a wooden skewer or a toothpick inserted into the center of one comes out clean, about 12 minutes for mini muffins or 15 minutes for standard muffins.

- Remove the muffins from the oven and cool them in the pan for 5 minutes, then remove them from the pan. Put the melted butter in a small bowl and spread the extra 2 tablespoons sugar on a small plate. Dip the muffins' tops into the melted butter, then into the sugar to coat them. Cool slightly on wire racks before serving.

makes 24 mini muffins or
12 standard muffins

1¾ cups (9 oz/280 g)
all-purpose (plain) flour

2 tablespoons poppy seeds

2 teaspoons baking powder

¼ teaspoon salt

½ cup (4 oz/125 g)
granulated (white) sugar, plus
2 tablespoons extra

1 egg, beaten

¾ cup (6 fl oz/180 ml) milk

¼ cup (2 fl oz/60 ml)
vegetable oil

½ teaspoon almond extract
(essence)

2 tablespoons unsalted
butter, melted

makes 12
standard muffins

2 cups (10 oz/315 g)
self-rising flour

⅔ cup (5 oz/155 g)
granulated (white) sugar

½ cup (3 oz/90 g) ground
almonds

2 eggs, lightly beaten

1 cup (8 fl oz/250 ml) milk

¼ cup (2 oz/60 g) unsalted
butter, melted

1 teaspoon vanilla extract
(essence)

1½ cups (6 oz/185 g) fresh
or frozen raspberries

½ cup (1 oz/30 g) sliced
(flaked) almonds

2 tablespoons coarse
sugar crystals

raspberry-almond
muffins

Ground almonds give these muffins extra moisture and flavor. If you're using frozen raspberries, there is no need to thaw them first.

● Preheat the oven to 400°F (200°C). Grease 12 standard (½-cup/125-ml) muffin cups or line them with parchment (baking) paper liners.

● In a large mixing bowl, sift the flour. Stir in the granulated sugar and ground almonds. Make a well in the center.

● In a small mixing bowl, combine the eggs, milk, butter, and vanilla. Add all at once to the flour mixture, together with the raspberries, and stir until just moistened (the batter should be lumpy).

● Spoon the batter into the prepared muffin cups, filling them two-thirds full. Sprinkle evenly with the sliced almonds and sugar crystals.

● Bake until the muffins are golden brown and a wooden skewer or toothpick inserted into the center of one comes out clean, 15–20 minutes. Remove from the oven and cool in the pan for 5 minutes. Serve warm, or transfer the muffins to a wire rack to cool.

crumble-topped
apple muffins

For this recipe, use apples that hold their shape during cooking, such as Golden Delicious, Granny Smith, Jonathan, or Pippin.

makes 12 standard muffins

muffins

2 cups (10 oz/315 g) self-rising flour

1 teaspoon ground cinnamon

½ cup (3½ oz/105 g) firmly packed dark brown sugar

1 large apple, peeled, cored, and chopped

½ cup (3 oz/90 g) golden raisins (sultanas)

2 eggs, lightly beaten

1 cup (8 fl oz/250 ml) apple juice

2 oz (60 g) unsalted butter, melted

crumble topping

2 tablespoons unsalted butter, chopped

¼ cup (1½ oz/45 g) all-purpose (plain) flour

1 tablespoon firmly packed dark brown sugar

1 tablespoon shelled pumpkin seeds (optional)

- Preheat the oven to 400°F (200°C). Grease 12 standard (½-cup/125-ml) muffin cups or line them with parchment (baking) paper liners.

- In a large mixing bowl, sift together the flour and cinnamon. Stir in the brown sugar, chopped apple, and golden raisins. Make a well in the center.

- In a small mixing bowl, combine the eggs, apple juice, and butter. Add all at once to the flour mixture and stir until just moistened (the batter should be lumpy). Spoon the batter into the prepared muffin cups, filling them two-thirds full.

- For the crumble topping, in a small bowl, rub the chopped butter into the flour until it looks crumbly. Stir in the brown sugar and, if you like, the pumpkin seeds. Spoon the topping evenly over the batter.

- Bake until the muffins are golden brown and a wooden skewer or toothpick inserted into the center of one comes out clean, 15–20 minutes. Remove from the oven and cool in the pan for 5 minutes. Serve warm, or transfer the muffins to a wire rack to cool.

cider muffins
with cinnamon-streusel topping

A thick sprinkling of streusel tops a pan of these quick and easy muffins.
The apple flavor is especially pleasing hot from the oven.

makes 12 standard muffins

streusel topping

⅓ cup (2½ oz/75 g) firmly packed dark brown sugar

3 tablespoons all-purpose (plain) flour

2 teaspoons ground cinnamon

3 tablespoons cold unsalted butter

muffins

1¾ cups (9 oz/280 g) all-purpose (plain) flour

2 teaspoons baking powder

¼ teaspoon salt

¼ cup (2 oz/60 g) granulated (white) sugar

1 egg, beaten

¾ cup (6 fl oz/180 ml) apple cider or apple juice

¼ cup (2 fl oz/60 ml) vegetable oil

● Preheat the oven to 400°F (200°C). Grease 12 standard (½-cup/125-ml) muffin cups or line them with parchment (baking) paper liners.

● For the streusel, in a small mixing bowl, stir together the brown sugar, flour, and cinnamon. Using a pastry blender, two knives, or your fingertips, cut or rub in the butter until the mixture resembles coarse crumbs. Set aside.

● For the muffins, in a large mixing bowl, sift together the flour, baking powder, and salt. Stir in the granulated sugar. Make a well in the center.

● In a small mixing bowl, combine the egg, cider or juice, and oil. Add all at once to the flour mixture and stir until just moistened (the batter should be lumpy).

● Spoon about 1 tablespoon of batter into each prepared muffin cup; sprinkle with 1 teaspoon of the streusel mixture; and continue to fill the cups with the remaining batter until they're two-thirds full. Sprinkle the tops evenly with the remaining streusel.

● Bake until the muffins are golden brown and a wooden skewer or toothpick inserted into the center of one comes out clean, about 15 minutes. Remove from the oven and cool in the pan for 5 minutes. Serve warm, or transfer the muffins to a wire rack to cool.

cheddar, herb,
and garlic muffins

You can use any mixture of herbs you like. Try the muffins the first time with a combination of oregano, parsley, marjoram, and thyme.

- Preheat the oven to 400°F (200°C). Grease 12 standard (½-cup/125-ml) muffin cups or line them with parchment (baking) paper liners.

- In a small frying pan over medium heat, melt the butter. Pour off and reserve all but about 1 tablespoon of the butter. Add the green onion and garlic to the pan and cook over medium heat, stirring, until softened, 3–5 minutes. Set aside to cool.

- In a large mixing bowl, sift together the flour and baking powder. Stir in the Cheddar cheese and fresh herbs. Make a well in the center.

- In a small mixing bowl, combine the eggs, sour cream, and reserved melted butter. Add all at once to the flour mixture, together with the cooked onion and garlic. Stir until just moistened (the batter should be lumpy).

- Spoon the batter into the prepared muffin cups, filling them two-thirds full. Bake until the muffins are golden brown and a wooden skewer or toothpick inserted into the center of one comes out clean, 15–20 minutes. Remove from the oven and cool in the pan for 5 minutes. Serve warm, or transfer the muffins to a wire rack to cool.

makes 12
standard muffins

$\frac{1}{2}$ cup (4 oz/125 g) unsalted butter

3 green (spring) onions, finely chopped

1 clove garlic, finely chopped

2 cups (10 oz/315 g) self-rising flour

$\frac{1}{2}$ teaspoon baking powder

1 cup (4 oz/125 g) shredded Cheddar cheese

$\frac{1}{2}$ cup (1 oz/30 g) finely chopped mixed fresh herbs

2 eggs, lightly beaten

1$\frac{1}{4}$ cups (10 fl oz/310 ml) light sour cream

makes 12
standard muffins

$1\frac{1}{4}$ cups ($6\frac{1}{2}$ oz/200 g)
all-purpose (plain) flour

$\frac{1}{3}$ cup (1 oz/30 g) rye flour

2 teaspoons baking powder

2 teaspoons sugar

$\frac{1}{4}$ teaspoon caraway seeds

$\frac{1}{4}$ teaspoon onion salt
(onion powder)

1 egg, lightly beaten

$\frac{3}{4}$ cup (6 fl oz/180 ml) milk

$\frac{1}{4}$ cup (2 fl oz/60 ml)
vegetable oil

$\frac{2}{3}$ cup (3 oz/90 g) finely
chopped fully cooked ham

$1\frac{1}{4}$ cups (5 oz/155 g)
shredded Swiss or
Gruyère cheese

cheese-and-ham
rye muffins

For a satisfying light meal, serve these muffins with a green salad or a bowl of soup. Freeze any leftovers to reheat and serve later.

• Preheat the oven to 400°F (200°C). Lightly grease 12 standard (½-cup/125-ml) muffin cups or line them with parchment (baking) paper liners.

• In a medium mixing bowl, stir together the flours, baking powder, sugar, caraway seeds, and onion salt. Make a well in the center.

• In a small mixing bowl, combine the egg, milk, and oil. Add all at once to the flour mixture, together with the ham and about two-thirds of the cheese. Stir until just moistened (the batter should be lumpy).

• Spoon the batter into the prepared muffin cups, filling them two-thirds full. Bake until the muffins are golden brown and a wooden skewer or toothpick inserted into the center of one comes out clean, about 20 minutes. Open the oven, pull out the rack, and sprinkle the muffins with the remaining cheese. Bake until the cheese has melted, about 1 minute more.

• Remove the muffins from the oven and cool in the pan for 5 minutes. Serve warm, or transfer to a wire rack to cool.

sausage and sage
muffins

Italian sausages are typically made of pork and may be spicy or mild.
Any flavorful fresh sausage may be substituted.

makes 12 standard muffins

¼ cup (2 fl oz/60 ml) plus
1 tablespoon extra-virgin olive oil

¼ pound (4 oz/125 g) fresh Italian
sausage, casing well pricked

2 cups (10 oz/315 g) self-rising
flour

½ teaspoon baking powder

2 eggs, lightly beaten

1 cup (8 fl oz/250 ml) milk

2 tablespoons finely shredded
fresh sage leaves

● Preheat the oven to 400°F (200°C). Grease 12 standard
(½-cup/125-ml) muffin cups or line them with parchment (baking)
paper liners.

● In a medium frying pan over medium-high heat, warm 1 tablespoon
of the olive oil. Add the sausage and sauté, turning occasionally to brown
evenly, until cooked through, about 15 minutes. Remove from the pan,
drain on paper towels, and leave to cool. When cool, peel off the casing
and finely crumble the meat. Set aside.

● In a large mixing bowl, sift together the flour and baking powder.
Make a well in the center.

● In a small mixing bowl, combine the eggs, milk, and remaining oil. Add
all at once to the flour mixture, together with the crumbled sausage and the
sage. Stir until just moistened (the batter should be lumpy).

● Spoon the batter into the prepared muffin cups, filling them two-thirds full.
Bake until the muffins are golden brown and a wooden skewer or toothpick
inserted into the center of one comes out clean, 15–20 minutes. Remove
from the oven and cool in the pan for 5 minutes. Serve warm, or transfer
the muffins to a wire rack to cool.

bacon and
mushroom muffins

*Two popular breakfast ingredients help make these savory muffins
a wonderful accompaniment to morning egg dishes.*

makes 12 standard muffins

¼ cup (2 fl oz/60 ml) extra-virgin olive oil

2 green (spring) onions, finely chopped

2 slices (rashers) bacon, rinds trimmed and discarded, diced

3 oz (90 g) mushrooms, finely chopped, plus 6 extra mushrooms, sliced

2 cups (10 oz/315 g) self-rising flour

½ teaspoon baking powder

2 eggs, lightly beaten

1¼ cups (10 fl oz/310 ml) milk

● Preheat the oven to 400°F (200°C). Grease 12 standard (½-cup/125-ml) muffin cups or line them with parchment (baking) paper liners.

● In a medium frying pan over medium-high heat, warm the olive oil. Add the green onions, bacon, and chopped mushrooms and sauté, stirring, until softened, about 5 minutes. Set aside to cool.

● In a large mixing bowl, sift together the flour and baking powder. Make a well in the center.

● In a small mixing bowl, combine the eggs and milk. Add all at once to the flour mixture, together with the mushroom mixture. Stir until just moistened (the batter should be lumpy).

● Spoon the batter into the prepared muffin cups, filling them two-thirds full. Divide the extra sliced mushrooms evenly over the top of the batter. Bake until the muffins are golden brown and a wooden skewer or toothpick inserted into the center of one comes out clean, 15–20 minutes. Remove from the oven and cool in the pan for 5 minutes. Serve warm, or transfer the muffins to a wire rack to cool.

bacon, corn, and onion muffins

Fresh thyme leaves give these savory muffins a wonderful aroma and pretty appearance.

● Preheat the oven to 400°F (200°C). Grease 12 standard (½-cup/125-ml) muffin cups or line them with parchment (baking) paper liners.

● In a small frying pan over medium heat, melt the butter. Pour off and reserve all but about 2 teaspoons of the butter. Add the bacon and green onions to the pan and cook over medium heat, stirring, until the bacon is well cooked and the onions are soft, about 5 minutes. Set aside to cool.

● In a large mixing bowl, sift together the flour and baking powder. Stir in the corn kernels and thyme leaves. Make a well in the center.

● In a small mixing bowl, combine the egg, milk, and reserved melted butter. Add all at once to the flour mixture, together with the bacon and onions. Stir until ingredients are just moistened (the batter should be lumpy).

● Spoon the batter into the prepared muffin cups, filling them two-thirds full. Bake until the muffins are golden brown and a wooden skewer or toothpick inserted into the center of one comes out clean, 15–20 minutes. Remove from the oven and cool in the pan for 5 minutes. Serve warm, or transfer the muffins to a wire rack to cool.

makes 12
standard muffins

$\frac{1}{2}$ cup (4 oz/125 g) unsalted butter

3 strips (rashers) bacon, rinds trimmed and discarded, coarsely chopped

3 green (spring) onions, finely chopped

2 cups (10 oz/315 g) self-rising flour

$\frac{1}{2}$ teaspoon baking powder

1 cup ($6\frac{1}{2}$ oz/200 g) corn kernels

1 tablespoon fresh thyme leaves

1 egg, lightly beaten

$1\frac{1}{2}$ cups (12 fl oz/375 ml) milk

cornmeal mini muffins
with fresh corn and peppers

Fresh corn kernels cut right from the cob will give these muffins the best flavor, but you may also use drained canned or frozen corn.

makes 24 mini muffins

1 cup (5 oz/155 g) fine cornmeal (polenta), plus extra for sprinkling

2 cups (10 oz/315 g) self-rising flour

1 teaspoon baking powder

1 cup (6½ oz/200 g) corn kernels

½ small red bell pepper (capsicum), seeded, deveined, and finely chopped

½ small fresh red chile, seeded, deveined, and finely chopped

2 tablespoons finely chopped Italian (flat-leaf) parsley

2 eggs, lightly beaten

1 cup (8 fl oz/250 ml) buttermilk

½ cup (4 oz/125 g) canned creamed corn

¼ cup (2 fl oz/60 ml) vegetable oil

● Preheat the oven to 400°F (200°C). Grease 24 mini (¼-cup/60-ml) muffin cups; then, lightly sprinkle the cups with a little cornmeal, tilting the pan to distribute it evenly. Tip out any excess.

● In a large mixing bowl, sift together the flour and baking powder. Stir in the 1 cup (5 oz/155 g) cornmeal and the corn kernels, bell pepper, chile, and parsley. Make a well in the center.

● In a small mixing bowl, combine the eggs, buttermilk, creamed corn, and oil. Add all at once to the flour mixture. Stir until just moistened (the batter should be lumpy).

● Spoon the batter into the prepared muffin cups, filling them two-thirds full. Sprinkle the tops with a little more cornmeal. Bake until the muffins are golden brown and a wooden skewer or toothpick inserted into the center of one comes out clean, 12–15 minutes. Remove from the oven and cool in the pan for 5 minutes. Serve warm, or transfer the muffins to a wire rack to cool.

whole-wheat muffins
with fresh herbs

Serve these muffins instead of bread with soups, salads, or omelets.
They're also good spread with butter or cream cheese for a snack.

makes 12 standard muffins

1 cup (5 oz/155 g) whole-wheat (wholemeal) self-rising flour

1 cup (5 oz/155 g) self-rising flour

½ tablespoon baking powder

2 tablespoons snipped fresh chives

2 tablespoons chopped fresh parsley

1 tablespoon chopped fresh mint

1 tablespoon chopped fresh oregano

2 eggs, lightly beaten

1¼ cups (10 fl oz/310 ml) plain yogurt

⅓ cup (3 oz/90 g) unsalted butter, melted

● Preheat the oven to 400°F (200°C). Grease 12 standard (½-cup/125-ml) muffin cups or line them with parchment (baking) paper liners.

● In a large mixing bowl, sift together the flours and baking powder, returning the husks from the flour to the bowl. Stir in the herbs. Make a well in the center.

● In a small mixing bowl, combine the eggs, yogurt, and butter. Add all at once to the flour mixture and stir until just moistened (the batter should be lumpy).

● Spoon the batter into the prepared muffin cups, filling them two-thirds full. Bake until the muffins are golden brown and a wooden skewer or toothpick inserted into the center of one comes out clean, 15–20 minutes. Remove from the oven and cool in the pan for 5 minutes. Serve warm, or transfer the muffins to a wire rack to cool.

makes 12
standard muffins

½ cup (4 oz/125 g)
unsalted butter

1 small leek, white part
only, thoroughly washed
and thinly sliced

2 cups (10 oz/315 g)
self-rising flour

½ teaspoon baking powder

½ cup (2 oz/60 g) freshly
grated Parmesan cheese,
plus ⅓ cup (1⅓ oz/40 g)
extra for sprinkling

3 oz (90 g) fully cooked
ham, finely chopped

2 tablespoons finely
chopped fresh sage leaves

1 egg, lightly beaten

1¼ cups (10 fl oz/310 ml)
buttermilk

2 tablespoons sesame seeds

leek, ham, and parmesan muffins

Leeks have a subtle oniony flavor that goes well with cheese. Because the vegetable grows in sandy soil, take care to wash it thoroughly.

● Preheat the oven to 400°F (200°C). Grease 12 standard (½ cup/125-ml) muffin cups or line them with parchment (baking) paper liners.

● In a small frying pan over medium heat, melt the butter. Pour off and reserve all but about 2 tablespoons. Add the leek and cook over medium heat, stirring, until softened and golden, about 5 minutes. Set aside to cool.

● In a large mixing bowl, sift together the flour and baking powder. Stir in the ½ cup (2 oz/60 g) of grated Parmesan cheese, the chopped ham, and the sage. Make a well in the center.

● In a small mixing bowl, combine the egg, buttermilk, and reserved melted butter. Add all at once to the flour mixture, together with the cooked leek. Stir until just moistened (the batter should be lumpy).

● Spoon the batter into the prepared muffin cups, filling them two-thirds full. Sprinkle with the sesame seeds and the extra Parmesan cheese.

● Bake until the muffins are golden brown and a wooden skewer or toothpick inserted into the center of one comes out clean, 15–20 minutes. Remove from the oven and cool in the pan for 5 minutes. Serve warm, or transfer the muffins to a wire rack to cool.

whole-wheat muffins
with walnuts and pesto

For these muffins, use a mild-flavored oil, such as canola (rapeseed), corn, safflower, or sunflower seed oil, or a blended oil.

• Preheat the oven to 400°F (200°C). Grease 12 standard (½-cup/125-ml) muffin cups or line them with parchment (baking) paper liners.

• In a large mixing bowl, sift together the flours and baking powder, returning the husks from the flour to the bowl. Stir in the Parmesan and walnuts. Make a well in the center.

• In a small mixing bowl, combine the eggs, milk, oil, and pesto. Add all at once to the flour mixture and stir until just moistened (the batter should be lumpy).

• Spoon the batter into the prepared muffin cups, filling them two-thirds full. Bake until the muffins are golden brown and a wooden skewer or toothpick inserted into the center of one comes out clean, 15–20 minutes. Remove from the oven and cool in the pan for 5 minutes. Serve warm, or transfer the muffins to a wire rack to cool.

makes 12
standard muffins

1 cup (5 oz/155 g)
whole-wheat (wholemeal)
self-rising flour

1 cup (5 oz/155 g)
self-rising flour

½ teaspoon baking powder

½ cup (2 oz/60 g) grated
Parmesan cheese

½ cup (2 oz/60 g)
chopped walnuts

2 eggs, lightly beaten

1 cup (8 fl oz/250 ml) milk

¼ cup (2 fl oz/60 ml)
vegetable oil

⅓ cup (3 fl oz/80 ml) store-
bought pesto sauce

makes 24 mini muffins
or 12 standard muffins

⅓ cup (3 oz/90 g) unsalted
butter

1 fresh red chile pepper,
seeded, deveined, and
finely chopped

1 small red (Spanish) onion,
finely chopped

2 cups (10 oz/315 g)
self-rising flour

½ teaspoon baking powder

1 cup (4½ oz/140 g)
shredded Gruyère or Swiss
cheese

3 tablespoons chopped
mixed fresh herbs

2 eggs, lightly beaten

1 cup (8 fl oz/250 ml) milk

red chile, onion, and cheese muffins

To complement these muffins' spiciness and richness, you can use any mixture of fresh herbs, such as oregano, parsley, marjoram, and basil.

● Preheat the oven to 400°F (200°C). Grease 24 mini (¼ cup/60 ml) or 12 standard (½-cup/125-ml) muffin cups or line them with parchment (baking) paper liners.

● In a small frying pan over medium heat, melt the butter. Pour off and reserve all but about 2 teaspoons of the butter. Add the chile and onion to the pan and cook over medium heat, stirring, until softened, about 5 minutes. Set aside to cool.

● In a large mixing bowl, sift together the flour and baking powder. Stir in the shredded cheese and fresh herbs. Make a well in the center.

● In a small mixing bowl, combine the eggs, milk, and reserved melted butter. Add all at once to the flour mixture, together with the cooked chile and onion. Stir until just moistened (the batter should be lumpy).

● Spoon the batter into the prepared muffin cups, filling them two-thirds full. Bake until the muffins are golden brown and a wooden skewer or toothpick inserted into the center of one comes out clean, 12–15 minutes for mini muffins or 15–20 minutes for standard muffins. Remove from the oven and cool in the pan for 5 minutes. Serve warm, or transfer the muffins to a wire rack to cool.

blue cheese, pear, and walnut mini muffins

With their sophisticated combination of flavors, these little muffins are perfect to serve with drinks or as finger food at a party.

● Preheat the oven to 400°F (200°C). Grease 24 mini (¼-cup/60-ml) muffin cups or line them with parchment (baking) paper liners.

● In a large mixing bowl, sift the flour. Stir in half of the walnuts. Make a well in the center.

● In a mixing bowl, mash the blue cheese with a fork. Gradually stir in the milk, mixing until smooth. Stir in the eggs and butter. Add all at once to the flour mixture, together with the chopped pear. Stir until just moistened (the batter should be lumpy).

● Spoon the batter into the prepared muffin cups, filling them two-thirds full. Sprinkle the tops with the remaining chopped walnuts.

● Bake until the muffins are golden brown and a wooden skewer or toothpick inserted into the center of one comes out clean, 12–15 minutes. Remove from the oven and cool in the pan for 5 minutes. Serve warm, or transfer the muffins to a wire rack to cool.

makes 24 mini muffins

2 cups (10 oz/315 g) self-rising flour

1 cup (4 oz/125 g) chopped walnuts

4 oz (125 g) soft blue cheese

1 cup (8 fl oz/250 ml) milk

2 eggs, lightly beaten

1/3 cup (3 oz/90 g) unsalted butter, melted

1 firm but ripe pear, peeled, cored, and finely chopped

carrot-and-pineapple
whole-wheat muffins

With their savory-sweet flavor and pleasant tang, these fiber-rich muffins make a great lunch or dinnertime treat.

makes 12 standard muffins

7 oz (220 g) canned unsweetened pineapple slices or chunks, drained, juice reserved

1½ cups (7 oz/235 g) self-rising flour

½ cup (2½ oz/75 g) whole-wheat (wholemeal) self-rising flour

1 teaspoon baking powder

1 cup (4½ oz/140 g) finely shredded carrot (1 medium carrot)

3 tablespoons finely chopped fresh Italian (flat-leaf) parsley

1 egg, lightly beaten

½ cup (4 fl oz/125 ml) milk

¼ cup (2 fl oz/60 ml) vegetable oil

● Preheat the oven to 400°F (200°C). Grease 12 standard (½-cup/125-ml) muffin cups or line them with parchment (baking) paper liners.

● Crush the pineapple in a food processor. Set aside.

● In a large mixing bowl, sift together the flours and baking powder, returning the husks from the flour to the bowl. Stir in the carrot and parsley. Make a well in the center.

● In a small mixing bowl, combine the crushed pineapple, egg, milk, and oil. Add all at once, together with the pineapple juice, to the flour mixture. Stir until just moistened (the batter should be lumpy).

● Spoon the batter into the prepared muffin cups, filling them two-thirds full. Bake until the muffins are golden brown and a wooden skewer or toothpick inserted into the center of one comes out clean, 15–20 minutes. Remove from the oven and cool in the pan for 5 minutes. Serve warm, or transfer the muffins to a wire rack to cool.

pumpkin-spice
oat bran muffins

Nutmeg's warm spiciness complements the natural sweetness of pumpkin in these wholesome and flavorful jumbo muffins.

makes 6 large muffins

10 oz (315 g) pumpkin or butternut or acorn squash, seeded, peeled, and cubed

2 cups (10 oz/315 g) all-purpose (plain) flour

1 tablespoon baking powder

1 teaspoon ground nutmeg

1 cup (5 oz/155 g) oat bran

2 eggs, lightly beaten

¾ cup (6 fl oz/180 ml) milk

¼ cup (2 oz/60 g) unsalted butter, melted

● Preheat the oven to 400°F (200°C). Grease 6 large (1-cup/250-ml) muffin cups. Line each with a 6-inch (15-cm) square of brown or parchment (baking) paper, roughly pleating it to fit it into the cups; or line them with parchment (baking) paper liners.

● Steam or microwave the pumpkin or squash until tender when pierced with a fork. Leave the pumpkin to cool, then mash it. Set aside.

● In a large mixing bowl, sift together the flour, baking powder, and nutmeg. Stir in the oat bran. Make a well in the center.

● In a small mixing bowl, combine the eggs, milk, butter, and mashed pumpkin. Add all at once to the flour mixture and stir until just moistened (the batter should be lumpy).

● Spoon the batter into the prepared muffin cups, filling them two-thirds full. Bake until the muffins are golden brown and a wooden skewer or toothpick inserted into the center of one comes out clean, 25–30 minutes. Remove from the oven and cool in the pan for 5 minutes. Serve warm, or transfer the muffins to a wire rack to cool.

index